BEATRICE SH
A GIRL WITH GRIT:

BORN IN 1909 SHE SAVED OUR PILOTS IN WWII. GAINED A GOLD STAR AT BROOKLANDS RACING BIKES & CARS AT 100MPH! WAS A STEM PIONEER BEFORE HER TIME WHILE FIGHTING FOR EQUALITY IN A MAN'S WORLD. BEATRICE *'TILLY'* SHILLING DID IT ALL!

ELSIE O'NEILL

A well-researched record telling how one young girl was determined to follow her dream and succeed in a male dominated world. An encouragement for all girls so inclined to pursue a STEM career.

David Woodford, Beatrice's nephew
February 2021

Praise for
Beatrice Shilling – A girl with grit!

Women have always been powerful, but men tended to write history and forget about the contribution females made to our world. Determination is what kept them going and Beatrice certainly showed what women can do in man's world. She is amazing – from racing cars and bikes to saving the lives of our airmen in WWII.

Men have a lot to answer for, then and now!
Tony Ashridge *Author*

****

Written in a very gossipy manner with Jessica narrating, there are very sound and amusing links between the girls; their love of bikes and the need to succeed, but also their differences. Amazing photographs supplement the text which goes a long way to showing how Beatrice worked exhaustingly hard to gain the success she deserved.

I love the modern outlook on STEM and how sad that gender issues in science, technology, engineering and maths were an issue 100 years ago and still are today! *Such a disgrace in 2021.* Make a move to change that, girls.

A.P.B. *Single Mum, Teacher and modern feminist*

****

A great book for STEM fans, those who love strong women in history and 'girls with grit'.

HGM *Grandad and amateur local historian*

It hits the mark in many ways. Introducing different subjects such as International Women's Day – I didn't know there was one! Also the former Brooklands racing track, now a place of expertise for STEM enthusiasts and much more makes sound reading for both knowledge and interest. It is essential for todays *'Tweens and Teens'*.

The superb photographs, the background information with a few notes on family life as well as excellent text make it a comfortable read, pulling you in without being too heavy on the history side, yet gets several messages across.

Equality for all is essential, but importantly you can succeed with determination, hard work and building on those first steps and early experiences.

M McK *Teacher*

****

As a stay-at-home Dad, I have been reading this to my 10 year-old twins each day. I am enjoying the history being revealed about Beatrice – new to me – while my son and daughter are asking lots of questions about different aspects brought up in the book. I had to search the garage for a washer and find a 3d bit online!

How lucky to be able to do so many activities, but then again Jessica's savings from modelling and acting – *real work* – pay for it all. A good lesson to my two and others, who tend not to think about the actual cost of hobbies and sports etc. never mind how hard Jessica works as a child – her choice.

Lots of short chapters make it easy to put down and pick up again, along with a detailed Glossary and Bibliography.

Bill Y *Dad to Josh & Willow*

Beatrice was incredible and can teach us all a few things about life being unfair, 100 years ago and now! I need to catch up on STEM, equality for women and what my kids must do towards their future! Freda D *Granny and lover of local history*

My girls are extremely interested in famous women, gender issues and equality for all, especially in the world of STEM: they all scratch an itch or two. They are blessed that their school leads the way in ensuring all pupils have a sound grounding in those subjects as well as the expected curriculum.

Beatrice Shilling's fame was unknown to us. My parents were unaware of her, so the book has educated the whole family. I have not found any others books on Beatrice suitable for the 10 – 16 year group, also adults. *In fact, I have not found any of this ilk!*

I've managed to get the boys to scan read it! They love the history side of Spitfires and Hurricanes, but never realised women could be so empowering, stroppy at work (at home, yes) and above all, resourceful.

Riding motorbikes and racing cars, fiddling with the engines and saving our pilots in WW2 was surprising to us all. Well done, B! JW *Mother of four and Midwife*

To those who read, reviewed, offered advice and provided detailed comments about the book, thank you so much.

You are amazing!

Elsie O'Neill

B.Ed (Hons) MSc.

DEDICATION

To Jessica and Bertie for the hours of pleasure you bring me.
Your love of life and energy, even if exhausting at times to
your old Grandma!

To Dennis Lock & David Woodford.
Thank you for giving so much of your time, knowledge and
photographs.
I could never have written this book without you both!

Also to G, I, J and T for all their help and support.

It is very much appreciated.

Much love to you all.
Grandma Elsie
xxxxxxx

CONTENTS

Hi, I am Jessica!

Four years ago, I was faced with a dilemma or two!
Several big decisions to make that could affect my future.
Should I give up filming for the Red Cross or acting in general?
Was the slog and hard work really worth it all?
Beatrice also had major difficulties in her lifetime as well.
We are both 'girls with grit' who believe in equality for everyone.
Read on to find out more about what else links us together.

What? A unicycle for Christmas!

Grandma Swagg (GS) is always telling me,

"You can do anything or be anyone you want, Jessica – just try!"

After all, I am not yet ten, so I have my whole life ahead of me. I used to be extremely shy, was bullied and felt worthless at times. A new school and my family helped tremendously. Being confident and celebrating your own successes is not about an over-inflated ego or being pompous, conceited or just plain big-headed. It is accepting we all can do something in life and be proud of it. *Take those first steps and don't look backwards.* If the 'Mafia' at my previous school could see me now!

I adore school, almost everything about it including my friends, but this time last year I had a passion to do something very special, just for me. A passion that totally overwhelmed me. A passion that made my heart sing. A passion that kept me fit and increased my determination to succeed. My passion was to ride a bike, but not just any old bike, it was my unicycle! *I am actually quite discerning.*

Appropriately for a special present, or perhaps inappropriately due to the weather and time of year, my unicycle appeared at Christmas; a great surprise to me, but also a bit of a worry that made me slightly anxious, although nowadays I am generally a plucky character, who is not normally jittery in any way. When would I fit it in around all my other activities? *I had a film to make for starters.*

How on earth was I going to manage to ride a one-wheeled bike with two pedals, a frame and a seat? The key differences between this and a normal bike are the lack of a second wheel and no handle bars to grip or brakes! *YIKES!*

Apprehension was creeping in slowly. It was December, so there was no way Mum and Dad would permit me to try it outside regardless of my desperation to overcome initial fears. Still, I was determined to dispel any doubts bouncing around in my brain and convinced myself to be more optimistic about riding my unicycle.

Curiosity got the better of me, so I tried balancing on my unicycle, but kept toppling over, just managing to save myself from hitting somebody or the wall! Being almost stationary on a unicycle is not a good idea. You need to pedal to keep it upright or learn to idle – so you can guess the state I got in, even with my arms dithering and flapping like the squabbling starlings on the bird feeder.

How can I ever learn to ride my unicycle?
© GV

Dad said we'd all need chainsaw safety helmets complete with high impact visors and ear protectio as protective body gear to avoid getting banged and bruised, so we had a good giggle about it.

When I am older I will need all that protective gear as I would love a **Norton Commando** or I might even settle for a **BSA** like my Great Grandad's. I'll probably do without a sidecar like his.

However, that is many moons away – another one of Grandma's sayings when I ramble on about motor bikes. It also reminds me that I have many more push bikes to ride before then, but the first steps are important ones.

My dream bike a Norton Commando

Back to Christmas Day! I was building and coding with **LEGO WEDO2,** a great **STEM** kit when my little brother, Bertie, who was playing with **Stickle Bricks**, gave me an envelope. A rather wrinkled and slightly squashed purple envelope with gold stars emblazoned around my name. I wondered what it was, perhaps another Christmas card. Confusion as to what it might be had me currently blinkered. You will never guess what was inside it.

WOW! Unicycle lessons with an experienced circus skills lady in Portsmouth! I stammered a *Thank you* to Mum and Dad. Maybe I had some chance of success in the not too distant future. Mum and dad would pay for five lessons, but the rest would be covered by my acting and modelling fees, which tended to pay for dancing, singing and other activities I did. *The remainder was saved for a Norton.*

Sadly, it wasn't quite that easy. How could I wait? I was desperate to learn to ride my new bike. Grandma is always saying, *"Patience is a virtue, you have to learn to wait!"*

Although I was temporarily distracted by the smell of dinner, I dreamily thought of somebody who was born a few miles away. B raced bikes and cars; had to be patient, determined and not give up. *Determination was my middle name, so I wouldn't give up either!*

3

The Shillings girls and Mum – Beatrice on her lap with one bare foot!
I have to be different even as a baby!
©David Woodford

Allegedly, Mum's heritage can be traced back to **Sir Lancelot du Lac**, supposedly one of King Arthur's Knights of the Round Table and possibly of Irish, Welsh or even German descent. *It sounds French to me, so I'll go with that!* Her maiden name was Dulake, which may well be an anglicised version of du Lac.

WOW! Fact or fiction? Who knows?

Read on to find out more about Beatrice and her family – she was amazing! I am in awe of her and a great fan, too.

Do you admire somebody famous?

Do you admire anyone famous? There's lots of people out there to admire – pop singers, film stars, footballers and experts of all sorts. I am very fortunate to have worked with or met some famous people like Davina McCall from **This Time Next Year** fame – I'll tell you about others later – but the one I really admire is *Beatrice Shilling*, who actually lived locally to me, but sadly before my time. In fact 100 years before I was born, so that is kind of special. *Let me tell you her story – she had an amazing life and was a God-send during World War II.*

In between, I'll mention a few things that come to mind and towards the end of the book I'll update you on my musical theatre exploits and unicycle challenge. Chatterbox is my middle name and consequently, I do a lot of that and *'brain sparking'* when ideas or thoughts come to mind. I also side-track into other linked subjects as my mind cartwheels around, but I'll try to not do that too much.

You must have noticed by now how I do go on a bit!

Beatrice (B) was born on Monday, March 8, 1909 at 4 Sidney Villas, London Road, Waterlooville, in Hampshire. It was the 67th day of the year and a day that would go down in history a century later. Beatrice was Annie Shilling's third child, Nora Alice being four at that time and Gladys Nancie three. Mum, Annie (née Dulake), called Nancy by friends and family reputedly came from a semi-famous family way back in time. *(See the previous page, please.)*

Beatrice's Dad, Henry, who was fifty-two when he married Annie, was considered an old dad. He was previously a farmer before becoming a master butcher. Henry owned and employed staff in his fishmongers, butchers and game shops at the time when Waterlooville was a just a small village and considered a backwater *'over the hill'* from Portsmouth.

Waterlooville 1906
©Francis Frith

Today, Eric Jacksons, an electrical installation company, first established in 1928 is run by the third generation of Jacksons at 4 Sidney Villas. It is currently the oldest business surviving in Waterlooville and is still in the same premises as the Shillings' former enterprises. *Coincidentally, the Jacksons were operating their business around the same time Beatrice was nineteen and working for Margaret Partridge installing electrical equipment. They had other common interests, too, which you can investigate shortly.*

The Jackson's electrical contractors and supplier premises at 4 Sidney Villas
© GS 2020

In 1928, Eric was a founder member of the Waterlooville Motorcycle Club, still in existence today. Along with other interested men, it was set up after a suggestion by the local vicar. Something worth recalling when you explore Beatrice's history later in this book.

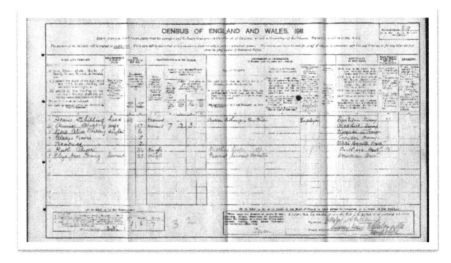

© Census 1911

The 1911 Census document detailed the names and occupations of those living in the Shilling family household at that time. Henry, aged 59, was listed as a '*Butcher, Fishmonger and Game* Dealer*'. He was head of the household and employed two people: Eliza aged 23 did domestic duties and Ruth aged 24 was a 'Mother's Help' with the children.

Their address was given as Sydney House Waterlooville.

His wife, Annie was 37 years of age, Nora was 6, Gladys 5 and Beatrice 2.

*A Game Dealer would have sold deer (venison), duck, partridge, rabbit, hare, pheasant, grouse, wild boar and squirrel. Game is usually any meat from a hunted animal rather than that raised on a farm.

The Shilling girls, and Oh, Dad, too!

Confusion arises when we anticipate the Shilling girls' names and who is who! Mum Annie, *known as Nancy*, was quite fortunate to have a domestic servant; 23 year old Eliza Jane Young came from Horndean, only a few miles north of Waterlooville. As well as Eliza, Annie (Nancy) also had a mother's help/nanny in 24 year old Ruth Pryer from Southsea.

Southsea is approximately 12 miles away via the old London Road that literally ran from Portsmouth to London and back. It was a famous Victorian seaside resort with train connections to London. Queen Victoria regularly stopped off here on her way to Osborne House on the Isle of Wight (IOW).

Local streets are named after her family, too. Portsmouth itself was also a naval base with a famous dockyard. Today it berths cruise ships, cross channel and IOW ferries as well naval ships in the working dockyard, including HMS Elizabeth, the navy's newest ship.

Southsea Seafront and Clarence Pier 1900s

For long distance travel, most people in the early 1900's used trains, but for shorter distances, horses and trams were more common. Ruth possibly took a train to Cosham from Southsea followed by a horse-drawn bus to Waterlooville. She may even have boarded the Horndean Light Railway tram as pictured here.

© *JJMarshallsay 2020*

In 1906 the cost was 1d (one old penny) from Cosham to the top of the hill where it terminated at the George Pub in Cosham, or 2d from there to Purbrook, near Waterlooville. For 5d (2p approximately today) she could go all the way to the terminus at Horndean, Eliza's village, but this was a little further than Waterlooville.

Ruth was responsible for the three children, so it appears the Shilling family were quite well off and fairly middle class.

The family moved around quite a lot but mostly between Surrey and Hampshire. Annie (Nancy) was born in Redhill Surrey while Dad, Henry, in Surbiton. *(Census 1911)*

Their first daughter, Nora Alice had been delivered in Kingston on Thames, while Gladys Nancie, known as Anne, was born in Croydon and Beatrice, always called Baby or B, in Waterlooville. As an adult she was also nicknamed Tilly! Find out why later.

Can you get your head around it? Don't worry, it took me some time, too, to sort out who was who!

I can't imagine doing all that moving around without a car and a removal company or van to shift our belongings, but on reflection, even though the Shillings were well off, they would not have had the possessions we do today.

Can you visualise life without a TV or technology equipment? Mind you, they had bikes. Very important possessions. Every girl and boy should own a bike!

Showering twice a day, nocturnal hair washes and changing clothes on a daily basis are a must in our household, but it would have been very different in the early 1900s. When I recall what I take to

Beatrice aged four © Dennis Lock

school each day compared to what little the Shilling girls would have taken then my mind boggles. Did they have to wear the same clothes every day even when Spanish 'flu hit in 1918? Was school cancelled? *(It was!)*

Incidentally, Gladys hated her name and according to her husband, Dennis Lock, never forgave her parents for bestowing that name. However, she was always called Anne, her mother's real name, and responded to that rather than Gladys.

Dennis, who was 23 years younger than Anne, married her in 1953 without any disagreement from the Shilling family.

Henry was rather old at fifty-two when he married Anne in the first place so would have been about 100 had he still been around in 1953. Recently Dennis told Grandma,

"(Gladys) Anne, whom I married in 1953 when we were 23 years apart in age, had always said she never forgave her parents for calling her Gladys. Everyone called her Anne. She signed official letters as Nancie. Anne died aged 103 in 2009. Anne had a full and interesting life, ballet trained and at one time stage assistant to famous illusionist Jasper Maskquelyn. Anne later obtained a London bachelor's degree in botany and chemistry."

A clever lady indeed. He also speaks highly of the family, especially his mother-in-law Nancy.

"Anne's mother (Nancy) was the sweetest, most generous lady and she supported our marriage (all our families did) in spite of the age difference. Henry Shilling, a crack shot at Bisley, (firing range) died before I met the family."

Beatrice's Mum, Nancy on her bike around 1900 © Dennis Lock

Did Beatrice's initial interest in bikes stem from her Mum, Nancy? What an elegant looking lady with her long dress and bicycle. I bet it wasn't easy to ride with such a beautiful flowing dress.

WOW! Although I would love to have met Beatrice in person, I find it amazing that her brother-in-law, Dennis and nephew David have provided some personal memories and photographs of her family. I am greatly indebted to them both for an insight into the Shilling girls and family.

The Shilling family returned to Surrey in 1914 when Beatrice was five and eventually she went on to Surbiton High School with her sisters where Beatrice was still known as B.

"Everyone in the close family called Beatrice simply 'B', which is how she signed family letters." Dennis informed Grandma.

By 1920 the girls attended a grammar school in Dorking, where evidence of B's determination, temper and short fuse was demonstrated daily to the staff. In a letter to her husband, George, Beatrice confirms that her behaviour at school did not match her achievements in quality, while he appeared a more pleasant pupil.

"I don't think you were naughty enough at school – I was ticked off many times a day at school. I used to look so miserable that they used to apologise for talking so harshly. If you could establish that if you got ticked off you burst into tears you could get away with anything." (in Freudenberg 2003)

I'm off to church this morning – Pentecost – therefore no unicycling or dancing until later. Grandma insists I go every so often when it fits in around the other things I do, but I'll explain later how my busy days go and how it impacts on my time. *It's frenetic!*

Church got me thinking: I wonder did the Shilling girls have to attend church? If so, it doesn't sound as though it improved B's attitude and behaviour.

Grandma explained that long ago, in her day and before, how the church congregation and ministers often put the fear of God's wrath in children, so they generally did behave.

She remembers it well!

All three Shilling girls achieved highly, not only academically but also in domestic subjects such as needlework and sporting activities. While Nora happily produced household items such as tray cloths, the other two girls much preferred to tinker around with tools and make artefacts from natural materials such as wood. Nora, in later life, also married and, according to her brother-in-law Dennis,

"Had three children, David, Janet and Marian. Nora was tall (unlike her sisters) but when she died had shrivelled pathetically owing to osteoporosis. She was a talented amateur artist and a very efficient mother and housewife."

David, Nora's son, recalls Beatrice with fondness.

"We loved our Aunt B. She was very close to my mother and my sisters and I benefitted."

Tinkering times

Like me, Beatrice enjoyed tinkering with Meccano, although her construction kit of perforated strips and angled brackets etc. were made from sheet metal or perhaps tin plated, while mine, 100 years later, is mostly plastic. I do have some older bits from the 1950s along with some instruction leaflets. It is much more solid than the newer plastic kits and sells for a fortune on e-bay and at auctions.

Frank Hornby, manufacturer of the famous trains invented Meccano around 1900. He ran competitions for model makers and also sold Meccano magazines for one (imperial) penny. I wondered if Beatrice ever competed with her models in that boys' world and was delighted to establish that she did. Apparently, Beatrice became so proficient with her Meccano construction kits that at twelve she entered, and won a prize in a national competition set by Meccano Magazine. Verity, from Waterlooville Library explained that:

"Beatrice's entry was a working model of a spinning wheel, inspired by seeing one in use at an exhibition she visited with her mother."

Meccano 1911/2 © www.alansmeccano.org

Roger Marriott very kindly found me the article in one of his treasured collections of Meccano Magazines (MM) from 1921/2.

"I have only been able to find one reference to Beatrice Shilling in the MM. She gained an "additional prize" in the 1920/21 competition begun in 1920 and published in the MM July-August 1921.

She is listed as 'Beatrice Shilling, 65a South Street, Dorking, Surrey; Spinning Wheel' in the section for competitors aged between 10 to 14 years of age.

There is no picture of the model and I cannot find any further mention of her."

Now that I had an exact date I searched the internet and found electronic copies of old Meccano Magazines including the July – August 1921/2 one in which Beatrice was mentioned. It is not very clear, hence the stars to identify her, but more proof of her win and skills at only twelve. *David, her nephew was thrilled to have a copy.*

I was delighted to hear this from Roger as I did wonder if she was excluded from any write-up being female, or if in fact, it was a local dealer's competition she had participated in. Roger also told me about a local event at that time; surprisingly a Meccano Club for girls!

"There is a note in Sept/Oct 1921 of a club in Claygate, Surrey of the formation of a girl's club to complement a boy's also running at this time but it does not seem to be close to Dorking, and there is no mention of members."

Thank you, Roger, you are amazing tracking this all down for me.

It got me thinking. I wondered if there are any Meccano clubs locally running today and if they are female only! Back to the old iPad to search them out.

Seconds later – isn't the internet fantastic? I came up with one a few miles away; The Solent Meccano Club, which has been running for thirty years with free membership and local events held six times a year in village halls (pre- Covid-19). Now that would have suited Beatrice if local to her in Dorking, but sadly none at that time in her area. Apparently, the clubs are worldwide as far afield as Australia and Argentina!

I, too, enjoy being creative whether it is designing with fabric, cooking, clay, making objects or fiddling with my Lego, screws and nuts, but hoping to end up with something that moves, though I am not quite up to Beatrice's standards, *yet*. I am also not **ambidextrous** like Beatrice, as David her nephew explained.

"Beatrice would change hands with her pencil when going from the right to left side of a piece of paper."

You try it, it really is quite difficult to do and produce an accurately formed image using both hands, but it must have been so useful later in life when dexterity, speed and skill mattered most to B.

During an interview with Woman Engineer magazine Beatrice recalled her childhood. It seems she enjoyed mechanical engineering even then. I'm in with a chance, but knives are out!

"As a child I played with Meccano, I spent my pocket money on penknives, an adjustable spanner, a glue pot and other simple hand tools." (www.bbc.co.uk/news/uk-england-manchester-40267364)

Not that I'd be allowed a penknife, but I certainly love science, and other *STEM subjects at home and school. I enjoy trying to repair, improve or make items using those skills. Meccano is another favourite where I can get to grips with my tools.

Sorting the basics of my bikes requires a few of those talents, too. However, talking of bikes, I am becoming much more confident riding my unicycle, but nevertheless still have a long way to go to perfect my skills. Our driveway wall is useful to lean against when wobbly!

*STEM – science, technology, engineering and maths – please see glossary for more detailed information; also STEAM. Check out the **Stemettes**, too.*

You may hasten to ask, what other things do I enjoy or *have to do?* I have enjoyed performing arts from a very young age, starting ballet at four as well as drama and singing from six. I trained at the prestigious Sylvia Young Theatre School in London for two years between six and eight years of age, followed by the Guildford School of Acting from eight to eleven. More recently I set my sights high by auditioning for both *"Annie"* and *"Matilda"* in the West End.

Trampolining springs to mind as does sailing and paddle boarding; also violin – *YUCK!* I prefer the didgeridoo. During Lockdown we all learned to play table tennis, but I also love my dolls. I can't see Grandma, except via Zoom and Face Time but creating clothes for them with her help is teaching me new skills. *However, I have a long way to go before calling myself any sort of expert.*

I also enjoy undertaking television and internet adverts and was very fortunate to write and record my own song for charity. I'll tell you more later on.

Paddle boarding in Barbados (2018) where I had a modelling contract

Sometimes, I have difficult choices to make. Should I do this or do that? Currently I am torn with dropping something to give me more time on my unicycle, but what should I give up?

If I stop modelling and acting, I will lose my coveted place with my agents and perhaps not receive any offers next year. I need to dance to keep fit and supple – helpful when cycling. *Dilemmas!* Once again I think of Beatrice never giving up, so I keep pushing myself as hard as I can. *Determination wins!*

Beatrice – the teenage years

At school in Dorking, engineering and things of a mechanical nature were certainly classed as *'boys' toys'* in that era, but Beatrice did not let that stop her. *A dilemma? No, she did what she wanted!*

Fortunately, at my primary school the Head runs a free Lego WeDo2 club and everyone in the juniors can apply. Ironically, just like Beatrice and a later friend, Sheila, only two girls were interested in the STEM side of things. Even then I had to persuade Emma to join me as we go home together with Grandma and it saved her Mum doing an extra school run each Thursday afternoon.

There is no doubt Beatrice was a very intelligent young lady, although lady-like is probably not a word used to describe her. Just like me, beyond dancing etc. I am a bit of a tom-boy and not always ladylike in my dress sense or activities, but well-mannered of course; the opposite to Beatrice by all accounts!

Royal Enfield ©Richard Red Devil Motors

By fourteen Beatrice, with additional finance from Anne, had purchased a second-hand motorbike; a two-stroke Royal Enfield on which she competed against her two sisters riding their pedal cycles. Anne occasionally rode pillion behind Beatrice.

Beatrice became adept at taking it apart and improving the reliability of the engine. Whilst doing so, she developed skills and knowledge about its mechanics and intricacies, possibly far beyond that of many lads of her age. All that fiddling around with Meccano, spanners and a penknife proved invaluable while tinkering about with her bikes to advance their performance. *Beatrice had several bikes in her life time and continued to defy conventions.*

Stripping and reassembling the rifles belonging to her father, Henry, was another of Beatrice's pastimes. According to Dennis, B's brother-in-law, Henry had been an expert shot as a young man, winning prizes in a variety of events. By all accounts, he was a skilled marksman. *Beatrice would follow in his steps later in life.*

Bisley in Surrey, where Henry honed his gun skills, has been the base of the National Rifle Association since 1890, but nowadays is also a Site of Special Scientific Interest (SSSI) due to a wide range of fauna and flora, so cannot be developed for building work. It is well worth a dander around if you are into plants and wildlife.

Later in life, Beatrice was also a crack-shot but at Camberley Pistol Club and very competitive in many ways: her favourite tasks and sports generally thought of as being suitable for only the male species at that time. *I don't think we would stand for that today, girls, would we? Equality is essential.*

Grandma believes only weak males are intimidated by and show anxiety in the company of strong females. I bet Beatrice, as an extremely intelligent and strong woman felt the same and by all accounts showed it, too. *Beatrice had an uncanny ability to do as she pleased and tell others what she thought, even if rudely done.*

A motivating female biker & Olympic cycling

Alfonsina Strada, an Italian cyclist came to mind. Another motivating, tom-boy, biking female, whom I'd have loved to meet, but sadly died in 1959 of a heart attack as she returned home after watching a bike race. *That was before even Mum and Dad were born.* She was one of only thirty cyclists to finish a 21 day race around steep Italian mountains even though 90 started-off together.

The following year, she was banned from racing as officials declared the Giro d'Italia was for men only. *REALLY!* I just cannot believe how prejudiced this whole gender issue was and still is today, although improving to a certain degree. Similar to Beatrice, she rode push bikes and motorcycles. Beatrice must have been aware of Alfonsina who was nicknamed, *'the devil in a dress'*.

However, her sheer determination did not make her hesitate one bit. She raced and held the speed record for 26 years!

Alfonsina 1924
©podiumcafe.com

This reminds me that determination is my middle name!
I will succeed! I will conquer my unicycle!

I would love a motor bike and preferably before I'm fourteen. WOW! Even off-road I'll need to have a valid motorcycle rider's licence and a current vehicle licence – no tax discs needed nowadays but the **Driver and Vehicle Licensing Authority** (DVLA) have a great database, so could check at any point that I am legal. Following that my bike would need a valid **MOT** test to show it was road-worthy never mind insurance and the compulsory, though very sensible, need to wear a helmet. I don't think my unicycle helmet counts, though! There is no way I'll be allowed anything before 16 and taking the relevant training then, too.

Unless, of course, I can find a privately owned couple of acres in which to ride it.

I bet Beatrice didn't have to meet all these regulations and I am sure there would have been plenty of country lanes or fields to compete with Nora's and Anne's bikes in and around the Surrey countryside.

The Roaring Twenties appears quite an apt name, though not linked to Beatrice's and her acquaintances' love of speed during the 1920s.

Beatrice riding her Matchless V/2, a 1928 Sports Model while at Manchester University (1929 – 1932). ©Dennis Lock

Women's intellect and skills are not inferior to men's!

By the time she was fifteen in 1924, Beatrice had firmly decided that her future lay ahead in engineering and sought an appropriate apprenticeship on leaving school in 1926. Margaret Partridge, who was a member of the **Women's Engineering Society**, provided Beatrice with a training opportunity in her electrical engineering company in Devon. Beatrice was employed by Margaret for three years installing wiring and generators as electricity was brought to homes and businesses in the out-lying River Exe Valley. Margaret's enterprising skills and sheer determination ensured additional sites were contracted, too, providing the 17 year old Beatrice, who, incidentally, should have been 18 for the *'apprenticeship'* in hand, with additional experience.

Margaret wearing her fur coat to the left of Beatrice
© https://ietarchivesblog.org/

As mentioned earlier, Beatrice was not lady-like at all. Matthew Freudenberg, in Beatrice's biography references Margaret Partridge's letter to her friend Caroline Haslett, Secretary of the Women's Engineering Society.

"I have managed to give Beatrice Shilling over a week's wiring work, and it seems to be turning out a great success. I really think she is a great acquisition to the firm – able to enjoy any new experience – and not in the least superior or blasé – the fault of the very young at times. She has a wicked joy in making all the YWCA (Young Women's Christian Association) hostel stand their hair on end by tales of her unladylike exploits when wiring."

For this, Beatrice earned twenty-five shillings a week – in decimal terms the equivalent of £1.25, which would appear to be worth considerably more today, but due to inflation £1 today does not buy as much as it did in 1927. Apprentices in Beatrice's time were lower paid in monetary terms (actual coins or notes) in relation to today. Nowadays apprentices rely more on technology and so expect to be paid better as the cost of living is high, too.

As time went by, Margaret was more than aware of Beatrice's potential, so persuaded her to apply to Victoria University in Manchester for a place to study electrical engineering. Should she give up working and a wage or struggle financially at university? A better education may provide an improved income in a more interesting situation later on. A dilemma and one we still face today.

Beatrice was one of only two females to undertake this pioneering course in 1929 and had to borrow the £100 needed for her fees. The National Society for Women's Services provided it free of interest, possibly via Margaret's influence and knowledge of Beatrice. A local girl, Sheila McGuffie, was the other innovative student, who like Beatrice did not find it easy competing in a man's world.

Beatrice and Sheila at Victoria College Manchester © Manchester University

Another friend, Muriel Shepherd (later Breed), whom Beatrice met while working at Ferranti during an eight week holiday job, matched B in her love of bikes and sense of humour. They shared a room in Muriel's parents' house, B teaching her maths and physics. This supplemented the girl's evening class tuition and helped her understand it better to pass examinations.

Beatrice's first degree wasn't enough for her, so after graduating in 1932 with a 2nd Class honours, she continued her education by completing a Master of Science degree in Mechanical Engineering. She followed this by becoming a Chartered Engineer.

© *Dennis Lock (in Freudenberg 2003)*

At that stage job opportunities were extremely limited, more so for a female in engineering, as it was still thought of as employment for men. *How dare a woman even contemplate doing skilled men's work regardless of aptitude and ability!*

Educated females were encouraged to become nurses and teachers, though not doctors or scientists, and certainly not engineers, positions reserved for the male species of this world at that point in history and for decades to follow.

For many years women were not allowed to vote either; their brains being thought of as rather fragile and incompetent to that of men and therefore unable to make such crucial choices as electing an MP. In 1917, women aged 30 and over were at last given the vote. Younger women were not allowed to vote.

Yet during WWI, between 1914 and 1918, an estimated two million women replaced men in employment, proving that women were just as capable as them. Possibly better in many cases. *Excuse my judgements, but gender issues can be quite irritating at times.*

However, the Second World War was just around the corner and women were again needed to do men's work when they were shipped off to fight as before. For a second time the female workers were expected to give it up once the war ended and the men returned. They were paid less, too!

Something Beatrice was not too happy about when she was further employed in a vital occupation a few years later.
Were males' egos too delicate to compete equitably with women who were just as skilled, if not more so, than themselves?

After all, many women work full-time, raise their children and still undertake the majority of household tasks, even today in this so called liberated world. Of course, Grandma has her rant about that, too.

"Only weak men are worried about competition from strong and dynamic women. Never let them bully you!"

Incidentally, even Henry, Beatrice's father, was not too enamoured with her chosen profession until she successfully wired a bedroom light with a two-way switch to enable him to have a control by the bed as well as next to the door! *Mum supported her, though.*

Abruptly my thoughts moved away from Beatrice as I was reminded of another one of my favourite activities as a 4 year old. I loved building an electrical circuit with crocodile clips, wires, bulbs and a battery to make lights for my doll's house and toy theatre made from a shoe box. *I do love STEM activities.*

I expect you have done the same in school during science lessons on electricity – completing circuits to ensure the bulbs, bells, buzzers and simple motors work. It was fun, especially when connecting to most control technology equipment such as making door mats with alarms, controlling merry-go-rounds and traffic lights etc. Did you enjoy it? I loved it!

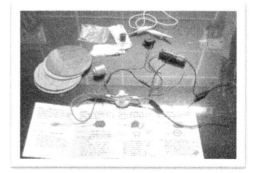

Part of our electricity kit & instructions but we explored rather than followed each step.

Pioneering women scientists and mathematicians who changed the world

I am almost certain Beatrice would have been aware of pioneering women scientists such as **Grace Hopper** born three years before her in the USA.

Grace Hopper Computer Scientist © Wikipedia

She tinkered with clocks as a child then went on to help the Navy decode enemy messages during WWII with her brilliant computing skills. Grace even became a Rear Admiral in the US navy!

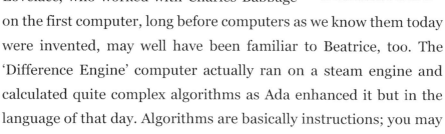

Rear Admiral Grace Hopper © Wikipedia

Awe-inspiring mathematicians such as Ada Lovelace, who worked with Charles Babbage on the first computer, long before computers as we know them today were invented, may well have been familiar to Beatrice, too. The 'Difference Engine' computer actually ran on a steam engine and calculated quite complex algorithms as Ada enhanced it but in the language of that day. Algorithms are basically instructions; you may know some from coding or maths.

29

Interestingly enough, *Ada studied birds to determine the perfect balance between body weight and wing size, but alas did not manage to soar into the tropopause – up to 10k high in the sky – never mind the stratosphere, approximately 30k up! However, flying was something Beatrice did eventually achieve.

Ada Lovelace © Alfred Chalon in Wikipedia

Every year, Ada is the topic of conversation to open an international celebration of the achievements women make in science, technology, engineering and maths. The plan is to highlight the importance of women working in STEM as well as encourage females to take up careers in that field. *That is us, girls!*

People meet and listen to others talk about their work and research, but in a very informal manner. In between, they **blog,** Twitter and Facebook to promote gender equality in engineering, education and the local communities across the world. Perhaps you could do it in a school **VLE** as a **forum** or **Wiki** with friends, get it checked and copy across safely. Maybe record a **podcast.**

Regardless, you can catch up on those wonderful women pushing the cutting edge of science to make a difference while changing the face of science, technology, engineering and maths. *We girls need to do it!*

*You may be interested to know that every year on the second Tuesday in October, Ada is remembered by a special STEM day – The Ada Lovelace Day (ALD).

Did Beatrice ever consider Formula One racing?

I wonder if Beatrice ever fancied being a Formula One driver like the Italian Lella Lombardie? During the Spanish Grand Prix in 1975, she finished sixth, the first female to do so in a World Champion race. These Italian women appear to be made of stern stuff and sheer determination in a man's world! *I intend doing the same!*

Lella Lombardi reading in the pit garage at Silverstone during a six hours race in 1976

© *Wikipedia*

Grandma believes that women's strength and ability should not be compromised, ignored or sneered at. Celebrate diversity and battle peacefully, but staunchly for gender equality.

Mahatma Gandhi believed that,

"Our ability to reach unity in diversity will be the beauty and the test of our civilisation."

We must never give up.

31

©www.matchlesslondon.com/blog

1931 Matchless motorbike and sidecar

Matchless bikes - made for the police force

Motorbikes and sidecars

Nevertheless, not to be deterred by male arrogance and stupid rules in the workplace, Beatrice decided to further her engineering

experience by investigating the behaviour of super-charged cylinder engines while working with a **Professor Mucklow** as his research assistant in Birmingham.

© *www.gracesguide.co.uk/*

While we're on the subject, her experience here helped Beatrice transform her Norton into a much faster machine, though not without problems on the race track. Prior to that, while at University, Beatrice was no newcomer to the race trials in the Peak District, driving motorcycles such as her Matchless V/2. *(See B's image page 23)* She even added a sidecar: something that could topple easily going around corners or if knocked carelessly. Sheila did ride in the sidecar at times but proved too light a weight to keep it positioned properly.

Motorbikes and sidecars are part of GS's childhood. Grandma remembers it with extreme clarity, when an aggressive drunk in a rather heavy Wolseley appeared from a side street in Newtownards hitting her Dad's Matchless motorbike and sidecar. They were lucky to survive the crash. *Beatrice never allowed accidents to stop her. Her thirst for speed was more important than a few broken bones!*

Can you just imagine what Beatrice would be doing if still alive and of working age in today's society? The mind boggles at all the possibilities. Would she be beating the current Formula One drivers such as Lewis Hamilton in his Mercedes and Sebastian Vettel steering his Ferrari around a race track? Perhaps she'd have arrived in space, her rocket knowledge being put to the test. I bet she would without blinking an eyelid at all.

Beatrice never abandoned her hobbies or old motor bike, continuing to tinker with the engine to improve its performance. Not only had she now got additional skills due to her engineering experience, but also a growing passion for motorcycles. During her time improving her education and throughout her early career, Beatrice began racing regularly on the famous Brooklands track in Surrey.

She made her dreams come true in a man's world. You can as well! Take those first steps ... Be determined – I am winning, too!

© *Brooklands Race Track Advert*

I have no intention of foregoing my dreams. I can unicycle, quite skilfully with growing expertise and confidence, too! It has been a very hard slog and will continue to do so. However, I need to keep at it to perfect my performance for somewhere very special.

At Southsea promenade

Brooklands was the world's first purpose built circuit especially for motor racing. Once again, Beatrice never flinched at embracing male competitors, this time on the racing track. She was a great exponent for women's liberation and a true *'suffragette'*, taking on men's roles and exceeding their ability, too. Beatrice never believed a woman had an inferior mind or skills to the men around her.

I never let a challenge inhibit me, and certainly don't believe the boys in my class are any more intelligent than I am. What I do concede, is that we all have different skills and abilities, so where I might excel at computing, literacy, dance and riding my unicycle – now slipping around the church hall as fluidly as a cat – a few boys are slightly better than me at maths and football, but only slightly, although they may think and boast otherwise. Is arrogance a male deficiency or just some of the boys I know? Belligerence is a common trait in a few of them along with some of their dads.

A child learns what it sees and hears ...

Grandma whittles on about celebrating our differences, encouraging diversity but above all learn what you can, be kind and thoughtful and think before you speak. Something Beatrice did not always do! She had a well-known reputation for speaking her mind, unkindly at times, too, as you will hear more about presently.

Over time Beatrice had upgraded her bikes to a **Norton Manx 500**. With some engine fiddling and her totally interchangeable hands, the now very experienced Beatrice managed to be the fastest female on two wheels at Brooklands. She achieved a speed exceeding 101 miles per hours (mph) while completing the 2.75 mile (4.43km) circuit in record time. B was awarded the prestige Gold Star for her performance: the envy of many males at that time for far exceeding their speeds at any time to date on that racetrack!

A Yorkshire Post & Leeds Intelligence article *(27.08.1934)* entitled, **"GIRL RIDER'S FEAT" 101mph on a Motor-Cycle at Brooklands** is even more impressive. It tells how Beatrice achieved her Gold Star lapping the track at 101mph. She finished third.

"Her sensational descent at 'the home of speed' came at the end of her annual holiday."

The judges were so impressed with her results they handicapped her in the next race, allowing a male to have a head start of 17 minutes and 16 seconds thus winning the race at a speed much lower than B's, a mere 82.18 mph! She missed third place by a yard (0.9144m).

It reeks of gender issues to me and poor male egos again! I bet the judges were men! Sadly, it was accepted by many at that time.

Beatrice raced and won from professional riders such as Noel Pope, born the same year as B, on his super-charged Brough Superior. Over time his bike became a legend while his ego was rather dented along with that of other males. *Being defeated by a female was not something he or other males expected.*

© *www.inventricity.com/tilly-shilling Beatrice posing for a Norton advert*

The Portsmouth Evening News reported on this success at Brooklands *(Thursday 27th June 1935, page 7)*

"Miss Beatrice Shilling, a 25-year- old Master of Science, won a motor-cycle race at Brooklands at 97mph, from famous men riders"

Not only was Beatrice a female, but in addition, an extremely clever person, who was winning to high acclaim in a male world.

Beatrice & George – Gold Stars abound

It is rumoured that Beatrice would not agree to marry her future husband, George Naylor, a mathematician she'd met at the **Royal Aircraft Establishment (**RAE) in Farnborough and on the race track, until he had attained the same Gold Star for equalling her speeds on the Brooklands track. It was 1936, but she did marry him two years later.

This ultimatum suggested that Beatrice may have had a dry sense of humour which could be witty and perhaps quite sarcastic,

too. Her nephew, David, reinforced this belief by telling me about their house in Farnborough.

"Early this morning I remembered Carfield was the name of Uncle George and Aunt B's house. Because it always had an old classic car in the run-in – a Lagonda and Fraser-Nash types."

George, during training in 1943, trying out a De Havilland Tiger Moth for size. He flew with Bomber Command carrying out numerous raids against the Luftwaffe © Dennis Lock

The Lagonda, pictured below, was modified and used on the racetrack as you will learn later. How funny to think that they thought of the driveway as a *'car field'* for storing old classic cars! Humorous and ironic indeed. It was just like Beatrice to be tongue-in-cheek for fun.

© *LAT Photographic Archive in Negative Gravity (2003)*

Beatrice driving the winning Lagonda Rapier at speed during the five-lap Lagonda race at Silverstone in June 1957

I believe the interior of their home was occupied by engines and other car parts during modification and upgrading. Joan Foster, their neighbour, friend and racing fan recently confirmed this.

"Bee & George Naylor lived seven doors away from us in Ashley Road, Farnborough before they moved to Cove. My father also worked at the RAE, in the radar department. My brother raced & we all went to meetings together. Their houses were always full of car bits & the dining room had a concrete floor to take the weight off their lathes!"

More recently their former home, Carfield, has been adorned with a Blue Plaque to mark B's achievements during WWII.

It was officially unveiled, followed by a buffet lunch celebration hosted by The Farnborough Society, on May 25th 2019. In addition, a display of photographs and text recalled Beatrice's wonderful and life-saving accomplishments.

© https://thefarnboroughsociety.org.uk/

The Channel 4 programme *Inside the Spitfire Factory* told Tilly's tale and showed the Blue Plaque unveiling along with interviews.

Judith Derisely, her God-daughter recalled Aunty B with fondness.

"She wore thick corduroy trousers and a man's shirt with a cigarette hanging out of her mouth. Aunty B bought me presents such as chemistry sets and microscopes – children's ones – but also the only teddy I ever owned."(Inside the Spitfire Factory:5 28.10.20.Ch 4)

Love letters during the War

It has been speculated that Beatrice's marriage was not a strong one, but enforced separation for three years during the war helped stabilise it, along with regular correspondence between George and herself. Her family would disagree; it was happy and fulfilling.

© *Dennis Lock*

Their letters do declare love for each other and how being apart was difficult. Both were extremely intelligent adults and there may well have been a competitive streak between them which could have caused a few problems, too, but *'darling'* and *'sweetheart'* were frequent endearments used regularly in their correspondence to each other. Matthew Freudenberg evidenced this in his book, Negative Gravity *(2003)* Romance was alive and kicking!

"Darling you know I love you very greatly, sufficient to encourage you in risking your neck in being a pilot or on a motorcycle more because I know you want to and will feel better if you are a pilot than because I want a pilot for a husband – you could become quite distinguished as a flutter-nark and stay a dart player for me.

All my love darling B"

Pressure of work at RAE, lack of sleep and George's training probably took their toll on both of them, never mind the dangers of war itself. B's unfortunate tone, too, could be mistaken in the short telephone conversations between them, but their correspondence throughout the war showed a deep affection and love for each other.

George's letter to B on Tuesday August 17th 1943 demonstrated his concern following their previous telephone call.

"I am worried, what was the matter with you tonight? I know that if we had been lucky we should have been together tonight and I should not be sitting up in bed writing to you now, I should be in bed with you instead ...

I love you more and more as time goes on and I miss you more and more as the days go by and I don't see you ...

© *Dennis Lock*

All my love, George"

In response Beatrice wrote,

"August 22, 1943

Carfield, Ashley Road, Farnborough

George dear,

If you write me letters like the one just before you phoned me twice last week, I shall start catching the train to Wolverhampton. Darling, it is a shocking business this being separated. I do hope to see you on Tuesday ...

I haven't seen you for 18 days, it is too long dear and between you and me I am going to make a job in Birmingham next week whether I see you or not this week ...

You know dear that I am too much in love with you to waste a 3 minute phone call being annoyed with you for going to a dance or something."

Being prepared to travel to Wolverhampton and Birmingham to be with George provides robust evidence of a strong relationship and love for each other even if a little turbulence caused unease at times.

There is no record of any children, and Beatrice was known not to be over fond of them, so both may have been more content in pursuing their personal interests in racing and working vocations or it just never happened. Children are expensive and time consuming, too.

George, in a letter to Beatrice, did suggest they would have to relinquish quite a lot to have children including Beatrice's career which she loved: their racing would be put on hold and they'd be broke for the next twenty years without her income never mind the expenses incurred in child rearing.

Beatrice, who had recently taken up flying appears to have made the decision for them.

Her body, her choice, her career at stake and again her sense of humour shows even if a bit more of a serious subject here. Writing to George she summed up her feelings aptly.

"I think all being well I'd rather have a Moth or a Magister (planes) than an infant. If I got a ground engineer's licence it shouldn't cost too much to run. Can I have one?"

Did she really have to seek George's permission or was she teasing?

However, at one stage she did have a retriever puppy; a great comfort, and sometimes a welcome substitute to many childless couples. But her nieces and nephew, Nora's children, were always welcome and they were very fond of her; admiring her skills and her ability to turn her hands equally to many tasks.

In another letter to George, Beatrice explains that she had been out horse riding with Nora's children on Christmas Day. She fell, bumped her head and was perhaps a little light-headed afterwards, but the experience left her in little doubt that children were not for her. I suspect it was the bump on her head rather than the children!

"26.12.43

Dearest George,

...incidentally, I am now finally and definitely decided that perpetuation of the race is a mistake."

Do you mind spiders? I have a great dislike of them although I know they are probably more frightened of giants like you and me! Beatrice detested spiders, so much so that she chased them with a blowlamp ensuring they were cremated quickly.

"There are plenty of pockets of resistance in this house occupied by spiders so I decided a flame thrower was the only thing for under the sink." (*In Freudenberg 2003*)

Beatrice's sense of humour is again evident here, nevertheless the cruelty to our native eight-legged mini beasts is quite uncalled for. Not even *I* would do that to a spider, although I abhor them along with woodlice and wasps, but maybe a few of the boys I know might if given the chance!

Courteous speech was not something that came easily to Beatrice. She had little respect for unnecessary rules, regulations or primness which did not go down well with her employers or bosses. Beatrice could be quite offhand, had a brusque manner and was often impatient with those whose standards and efforts were less exacting than her own. Although extremely clever and eventually reaching a senior position at the RAE, Beatrice did not go out of her way for advancement through being polite or thoughtful.

Had she sought promotion, Beatrice could have enjoyed leading her teams with a bigger pay packet to cover her expensive racing habit costs, never mind cigarettes. She was a very heavy smoker.

Critical of her superiors and being female did not predispose Beatrice to favourable positions of responsibility, but perhaps at times she preferred to be undertaking practical work and research rather than overseeing those under her from an office.

Beatrice told George,

"I tend to be too rude to my superiors or ineffective. I doubt if I'll ever get to the standard of some old hands ..."

However, she was promoted several times, particularly after her successes with carburettors and certainly deserved the recognition and additional pay, though received less than that paid to a male undertaking an equivalent job. *An extremely sore point!*

Beatrice was very much a *'doer'* and thought nothing of working late into the night – up to 19 hour shifts – far exceeding her normal hours to aim for a solution, but she also expected her team to do the same and was far from tolerant from those that abstained. Fish and chips rewarded those that did the additional nocturnal shift, also trips to the pub for a pint!

Judy, her God-daughter, also recollected that B, *"Didn't suffer fools gladly and there were too many fools around. B kept solutions simple while others made them complex."*

Beatrice adjusting her bike with George looking on. They were a team!
© Dennis Lock

Beatrice - racing was her life at speed!

Incidentally, following the **Motor Car Act of 1903**, Britain was forced to a maximum legal speed limit of 20 mph (32 km/h) on public roads, so Beatrice hit the speed on private land at Brooklands 5.3 times faster!

She almost killed herself at one point racing cars but had a hunger for speed.

Getting back to speed limits, there was concern that Britain's newly formed motor industry would be held back by their lack of ability to carry out sustained high-speed trials. On reflection, they needed Beatrice and her challenging need for speed to test them and lead the way forward!

Sorry, I forgot she was female – and females did not get asked to do something considered a man's occupation! GRRR!

Beatrice raced her Norton Manx until 1939, transforming it over time to improve performance and beat the lads. When war was declared, racing ended at Brooklands and the Norton was returned to a road machine to become Beatrice's chief means of transport for the next fourteen years.

I wonder what Beatrice would choose today – would it be a Harley or another Norton? Founded in 1898 they are now made in Donnington, Derbyshire. *What do you think? I'm still undecided.*

I have been fortunate to meet a couple of Norton Manx enthusiasts and try out their bikes for size. It was amazing!

WOW! How fortunate am I to be trying out a 1947 Norton Manx – 73 years old?

John, the Secretary of a local Norton biking group arranged for a few of his friends to meet us. Geoff, who also worked at RAE, has a 1947 Manx and Roger a 1957 bike, but in great condition for their ages.

They very kindly trailered them to do a photo shoot with me, but sadly it rained heavily, so we didn't get such good photos. However they loved showing off their incredible bikes and I had fun trying out both of them. *Thanks, lads!*

Both bikes – a 1947 and 1957 Norton Manx

Brooklands - the history in a nutshell

I mentioned Brooklands earlier as a favoured racing track of Beatrice and George. Today Brooklands is an aviation museum, housing examples of vintage cars, motorcycles and other forms of transport. Part of the former concrete track has been restored.

It originally opened in 1907 and held a 100 mile massed start cycle race. Road racing for cycles was not permitted on open roads at that time, so the Brooklands track was ideal: it was safe. By the 1930s cycle races were common place there. A first for Brooklands was the trials to select competitors for the World Cycle Championships to be held in Montlhéry in 1933.

© *Brooklands mass cycle ride*

By 1908 motorcycle racing began. Initially the numbers of spectators and participants were low, but over time this increased as did the speed of bikes and interest in racing.

Brooklands not only accommodated racing but also housed one of Britain's first airfields as it had been requisitioned by the War Office in 1914 for military use. By 1918, in addition to the racing track and aerodrome, it produced military aircraft such as the Wellington bomber, but also the Viscount and VC 10, both commercial planes.

During WWI Brooklands was used to test bikes for use in the armed forces as well as holding race meetings for service men at that time. Sadly it was bombed by the Luftwaffe on September 4th 1940. It caused a substantial loss of life and untold injuries to many present on the site at that point.

On re-opening following the end of the First World War, Brooklands was renowned for accommodating the fastest and best in motorcycle racing throughout the civilised world. Races such as the Hutchinson 100 mile and Brooklands 500 miles races were very popular events and eventually led to women being included by 1928.

An opportunity Beatrice did not pass by when older.

© *Dennis Locke in James Holloway (2020)*

David, her nephew, explained the above photo.

"Beatrice on her Norton having a push-start at Brooklands from her friend Muriel Breed." (Née Shepherd)

The last race at Brooklands was held by the Brooklands Automobile Racing Club on August 7th 1939.

© *Brooklands*

Refurbishing Brooklands – now STEM City

In 2015 Brooklands received a substantial grant from the Heritage Lottery Fund (HLF) of nearly £5 million to transform the listed Wellington Hanger into the Brooklands Aircraft Factory and restore part of the track to its former glory. It had been covered by an aircraft-hanger since 1940. This was removed, restored and re-sited. In addition, a plan to build a Flight Shed in which to store the museum's amazing artefacts of historic planes was enabled. Work has continued over recent years with private funding and a £1 million Government grant in addition to other donations.

www.bbc.co.uk/news/uk-england-surrey

The Earl of March re-opened a refurbished Brooklands on June 17th 2017. To relive the first opening in 1907 a re-enactment of vintage cars drove around the track to emulate the original procession.

The aim of the project is to encourage and inspire generations of young people to take up STEM subjects as well as train volunteers to restore historic aircraft sympathetically and accurately to their former glory. *Adventurous plans for Brooklands and the race track!*

One of the things I love about Brooklands is what they do for tweens and teens. You already know how much of a STEM fan I am, so I would love to undertake one or more of their events to further my skills. Currently not running due to Lockdown and Covid-19, they have workshops, one especially for girls to explore future job opportunities through studying STEM subjects and it is FREE!

You may remember Beatrice's link with the Women's Engineering Society (WES) – Margaret Partridge gave her employment and encouraged her to undertake a university degree, a start to her STEM career, though not known by that term then. At the Brooklands' day you can meet, work with and be inspired by current female members of the WES. There are opportunities to tackle some STEM activities and win Brooklands' prizes, too. *Lunch is included as well.*

In addition, they run a Saturday Science Club for any children 10-16 years of age who may be interested in STEM. The one I am attracted to is where you can build a Roving Robot over two weeks – a long way to go to Surrey for me, but it will depend on dates and my TV or dancing commitments. The Brooklands' website advertise it as an opportunity to;

"Build an analogue robot that uses line-detecting technology to move swiftly along a marked path. On the way you will learn about electronics, motors and circuitry. You will get to use a soldering iron, wire up the robot and even get the chance to decorate your robot in your own style." (www.brooklandsmuseum.com/)

I'm OK on basic circuits and using motors etc., but still fancy doing this. If not, I'll talk grandma into doing something similar but maybe without the soldering iron, though I know she has one.

We might need to upgrade Bertie's electricity kit, too. He loves using the motor to spin the cardboard circles we made to blend the colours: also making a complete circuit to light the bulb. His latest trick is remembering the colour coding of wiring up the buzzer and driving us all insane with its regular and incessant whine!

Grandma, I feel a trip to Brooklands coming on ...

*Bertie exploring some of the electricity kit – his preferred option is the motor used with spinners. You can never start too early on STEM (STEAM) activities. Another favourite STEM toy for investigating is **BRIO** – brilliant for developing thinking and exploring skills, too. He also loves simple coding with **Daisy the Dinosaur** on our family tablet and Grandma's iPad!*

Silverstone and Goodwood

Silverstone was the destination track chosen in 1935 by B to race her modified Lagonda Rapier. Once again, speed was part and parcel of Beatrice's way of life and she raced around exceeding 100 mph. By the time the Second World War broke out she had an exceptional reputation on the racing circuit, not only for motorbikes but also for racing cars such as her modified fixed head coupe.

Later, Goodwood at Chichester provided the main track for racing including their Austin Healey Sprite, similar to the image below. It was tuned and raced by Beatrice and George. *That was before the engine exploded and ended the car's life.*

© *www.sportscar2.com*

Sadly, Beatrice's car racing came to a hasty end following a crash which seriously damaged her legs and restricted the blood flow in her circulatory system.

This was no hindrance to George who carried on racing regardless of potential dangers and blown up engines!

Genetics at work

My Great Grandad, Bobby, loved bikes and cars with a passion. He was the first to travel the length of the newly opened M1 in Belfast on his BSA ZB31 bike in July 1962.

Like Beatrice, he previously had a Matchless.

Incidentally during WWII Matchless produced 80,000 G3 and G3L bikes for the armed forces!

Grandma recalled him telling the family that his speed exceeded 95mph as there was no speed limit imposed on the M1 at that time. *Fact or fiction?*

"The first user of the road was a motorcyclist, Robert McFall of Belfast."

(https://en.wikipedia.org/wiki/M1_motorway (Northern Ireland)

On your marks . . . Bob McFall, Highfield Drive, Belfast, warms up his machine in readiness for the "start." He was first on the motorway.

He was full of the thrill and excitement of being first on the M1 just a few days before her 9th birthday. At 37 Great Grandad even had his photograph in the Belfast Telegraph that night.

I have recently managed to track down a blog article on Fortean Ireland *(2019)* about Great Grandad. Grandma asked years ago, but the Belfast Telegraph was unable to locate the original photograph as their archives have moved outside the city.

I do question whether genetics and something deep in our family DNA has passed on this love of bikes and competitive spirit to all the boys, my uncles and me. The girls felt safer in cars – *what a let-down for women's lib!*

BSA ZB31

However, as an enthusiastic pillion passenger, minus a helmet *(not a legal requirement in those days)* and hanging onto a leather belt around his waist for many years, Grandma remembers their later escapades on his green, black and chrome BSA ZB31 as if it was only yesterday. *Grandad always wore goggles and a helmet.*

Beatrice, his senior, would have beaten him hands down doing a ton or more on her Norton even though she would have reached 53 years of age!

*Beatrice fine tuning
her bike
© Dennis Lock*

The war years – a genius at work!

Beatrice joined the **Royal Aircraft Establishment** (RAE) at Farnborough in 1936 as a technical assistant in the Publications department where she wrote instruction leaflets for the maintenance of the Bristol Pegasus engine.

Coincidentally enough, Great Grandad, an avid biker, also wrote technical documents but for IBM in the 1980s and linked to their computer systems.

In 1937 the Nottingham Journal reported that Beatrice, along with another female had been employed as *'Air Ministry recruits'* to their staff. This was regarded as something quite unusual for women, but what an achievement for women's liberation!

Nottingham Journal - Monday 01 November 1937, page 3

Air Ministry Women

One of the most interesting new developments in women's engineering is the more general acceptance of women on the technical staff of the Air Ministry. Miss Hilda Lyon has been appointed scientific officer at Farnborough, and Miss Helen Grimshaw has also been given a post on the staff. Miss Beatrice Shilling and Miss S. E. McGuffie are also "Air Ministry recruits."

Very quickly Beatrice became the leading specialist in aircraft carburettors. Edward Cameron, in The New York Times *(1910)*, described the carb as *'the heart of an engine'* and went on to say if it wasn't functioning correctly then the car would not work effectively. It was imperative to get it working properly and this was something Beatrice excelled at, even though it was taking time and patience to research, problem solve and aim for a successful result.

In design technology we are encouraged to explore *'trial and error'* to problem solve when making artefacts. Have you done that too? It is characterised by repeated, varied attempts, both practically and through design, which we continue until successful or give up to seek support; occasionally through lack of time in the school day.

Beatrice must have undertaken lots of trials and errors to improve the performance of her bike and in her research projects, at work. A bit like me and my unicycle – still hanging in there, but hard work and determination required at every point. *Substantial success is in sight – This Time Next Year – Davina, here I come!*

During the Second World War, Beatrice worked on a serious problem affecting the Rolls Royce Merlin engines which were fitted to the allied Hurricanes and Spitfires during the **Battle of Britain in 1940**. The British engines, unlike those of the German planes, which benefitted from a type of fuel injection, would misfire or cut out altogether when a pilot was diving steeply, often causing deaths. This force was known as **negative gravity or 'g'**.

As an **aeronautical engineer**, Beatrice understood that there was a fuel surge – too much entering the carburettor and flooding it – which caused severe problems and needed an urgent fix – the negative 'g' issue. The balance had to be perfected – enough to power the engine, but not too much to flood it. Float type carburettors relied on gravity to work effectively.

Beatrice, later nicknamed Tilly by fellow colleagues, but not to her face, and her team worked tirelessly to resolve the negative 'g' problem. She never gave up. It was a year in the making though not a final solution at that stage by any means.

Initially it was a cone shaped device that she created, but later, after thorough testing and still finding a few errors, it was redesigned.

Eventually she came up with the design for a simple but resourceful device; a small brass disc with a central hole or cavity, which when fixed into the engine's carburettor was able to induce fuel efficiency to the engine at the critical moment needed – the RAE restrictor.

Tilly's orifice example © gordanohomefront.wordpress.com

Too much fuel would flood the float chamber, but not enough restricted engine power and a safe flight. The correct balance was crucial. Fitting it herself at times, Beatrice travelled from airfield to airfield with other females to ensure it was correctly installed.

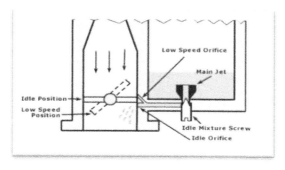

A simple diagram of the orifice in different positions

A great advantage was not having to remove the engine to do so.

It has been likened to a washer or a pre-decimal 3d bit coin with a hole drilled in the middle. It became known as Miss Shilling's or Tilly's orifice and after repeated testing – *trial and error* – demonstrated its effectiveness; an improved version was used on all allied aircraft with Rolls Royce Merlin engines.

A Supermarine Spitfire © wikiwand.com

Persistence towards perfection

Over time and further trials, it drastically reduced engine cut out and saved lives. It also meant that the British Spitfires and Hurricanes could dive and duck to avoid the German Messerschmitt 109s catching them in combat and therefore allowing the British to beat the powerful Luftwaffe. Beatrice didn't stop there, but continued to improve and develop the design in order to eliminate it entirely. Tilly, as she was nicknamed, was a fierce competitor, not only on the racetrack but also in the laboratory and no man stood in her way!

Maybe you have explored WWII in school, so recognise the names of these famous planes. There are still about 50 flying today for special events as well as those in military museums such as the Spitfire and Hurricane Memorial Museum in Ramsgate, Kent. The Hurricane fighter, first flown at Brooklands in 1935, is estimated to have been responsible for 80% of the enemy aircraft shot down in the Battle of Britain. One can be viewed in the Flight Shed at Brooklands. Amazingly, 20,334 Spitfires were built between 1936 and 1948, mostly to support the war effort.

Beatrice and her team must have been extremely busy sorting out their negative gravity problems in both Merlin engines.

Merlin engine © Peter Reese

By 1942 the approved adaptations with the RAE restrictor along with essential advice was saving lives and helping Britain outdo the German bombers. Beatrice spent many a train journey as far as Scotland, possibly to Abbotsinch and Grangemouth, supplying advice on engine carburettors and new developments. At last she was recognised for her contributions to the war effort, but only in a minor way. *One small step for womankind, but first steps are the start!*

In addition, planes were adapted for naval use on aircraft carriers. Initially, there had been problems with the Seafires missing the deck and going overboard or hanging by the catch wire when the hook hadn't engaged properly to stop the plane.

Later, Seafires *(named so from 'sea' and 'spitfire')* had folded wings and other adaptations to ensure the planes fitted their role at sea more precisely; they could be stored under the deck and play their part in saving lives. A number were Australia based where they undertook dog-fights with the Japanese *kamikaze pilots in the Pacific.

By 1945 Spitfires were engaged in several battles with the Japanese and succeeded in keeping them from invading India and Burma. They were used to drop 500 pound bombs at Sittang Bend in Burma resulting in 7,000 plus Japanese deaths compared to 95 British. Deaths were sad, but it appeared a necessary task to ensure our freedom from tyrannical extremists who would not talk peace.

Although I doubt that my prospects will be similar to Beatrice, I have taken my first steps towards my future. Who knows what lies ahead *Dilemmas galore: choices to make, but where will it take me*?

* Kamikaze pilots made deliberate suicidal crashes into ships or other enemy targets.

Did George challenge Beatrice to fly?

The **Tech-Flight scheme** at the RAE provided an opportunity for Beatrice to take up flying, logging some 200 hours but she never considered herself a worthy pilot. Being short at under five foot two, she had to build up the control pedals in order to reach them and this may have reduced her confidence slightly, although with racing that did not appear to be a problem. George, her husband, soared above her at over six foot.

A Yorkshire man by birth, he was a pilot in bomber command and flew for many extra hours during WWII, suffering from tinnitus – a hearing problem – and other medical issues in later life due to his flying. He was awarded and received the Distinguished Flying Cross for his acts of courage and bravery.

Gallant pilots like George, ensured minimal damage was done to imperative sites such as London, Portland and Southampton as up to seventeen squadrons were deployed to demolish the Luftwaffe bomber formations hitting Britain.

https://en.wikipedia.org/wiki/Distinguished_Flying_Cross_(UK)

Was learning to fly a challenge George set Beatrice in the same way she insisted he earned the coveted Gold Star medal for travelling at speed during racing at Brooklands?

Currently, Beatrice's medals, including her Gold Star, are on display at Brooklands.

Correspondence does not always receive the response you prefer

Sometimes letters, e-mails and Tweets do not receive replies or the outcome you would expect. In August 1937 Beatrice received a letter from the Chief Superintendent at RAE about an *'Acting Up'* position she was offered in the Engine Experimental Department. However, this was at a much lower salary than the one stated in the advertisement.

Just like me, I can hear you scream,

"Not fair, just because she was a female!"

Not fair indeed and Beatrice, being Beatrice, did not leave it there!

On August 11th 1937 she responded in writing to the offer pointing out the difference in payment for this Assistant Grade II post, a post she had been interested in earlier in the year. *However, the Superintendent was a man and men got paid more than women, so it probably wasn't an issue to him!*

By 1969 Beatrice finally became Head of the Engineering Division at the RAE. A long time coming for such a skilled female.

Today, we are still fighting for equality – the same pay for the same job regardless of gender, yet, hopefully in engineering some progress will be made as first class engineers are in short supply. *Women included!*

Medals or peace?

Grandma has her Dad's WWII and Grandad's WWI medals, but I'd rather have none and see war cease across the world. My acrostic poem, which I wrote for homework a few years ago, was to mark the centenary of WWI. *It shows how futile war is.*

100 WORDS FOR 100 YEARS CHALLENGE – WORLD WAR 1 POEM

Why do wars happen across the world even today?

Often innocent people are badly hurt – young children, mums, dads and ageing grandparents, too many die needlessly in the crossfire or by bombs

Rural country sides, busy towns, cities, villages, at sea, in the air, in the trenches

Languages speak hate not love

Disastrous, determined, desperate consequences for their actions

Wild animals can be hurt or killed by people's actions

Are wars worth fighting for – riches, religion, land and hate?

Recommendations to talk and not fight, but who listens?

1 world, too many wars, none of them are necessary – STOP NOW!

Jessica

The main *'fight'* I am interested in is equality for all, especially in STEM related opportunities!

I enjoy poetry, especially funny ones and those that rhyme, but sometimes we have to be quite serious and write about important subjects that matter in today's world. One thing is certain. *I'll never be a professional poet, though! Will you?*

Beatrice receiving her Honorary Doctorate from Professor Lighthill
at the University of Surrey (1969)
© *surrey.ac.uk*

Recognition for Beatrice – at last!

Beatrice continued to work for the Royal Aircraft Establishment until her retirement in 1969 reaching a senior post and receiving a medal – the Order of the British Empire (OBE) in the News Year's Honours List 1948/9 for her efforts during the war. King George VI was on the throne.

In 1969 she was awarded an honorary doctorate from the University of Surrey. Beatrice was also a chartered engineer and a member of the Institution of Mechanical Engineers, in addition to the Women's Engineering Society. According to the Engineering Council, chartered engineers, *(Wikipedia 2018).*

"Are characterised by their ability to develop appropriate solutions to engineering problems, using new or existing technologies, through innovation, creativity and change. They might develop and apply new technologies, promote advanced designs and design methods, introduce new and more efficient production techniques, marketing and construction concepts, pioneer new engineering services and management methods."

There is no doubt that Beatrice Shilling achieved that and more. She certainly deserved her honorary doctorate in December 1969 awarded by Professor Lighthill from Surrey University.

Goodness knows what I might achieve at Uni, but I certainly do want to go and do well with hard work and determination, but have fun, too! *I do hope to have my Norton Commando by then.*

Rockets and bobsleds

Back to Beatrice!

After the Second World War, Beatrice worked on a host of projects, including rocket fuel research, the ramjet engine, and the Blue Streak missile system. Its role changed to become the first stage of a satellite launcher, but was eventually removed from the space race due to costs. A few of the remaining rockets are held in museums, including the National Space Centre in Leicestershire.

1960s Woomera, Australia,
Blue Streak rocket testing
©@1steviekilne

In their spare time both Beatrice and George continued to race cars and motorcycles until their health prevented it. *At one point, she also lost a tooth or two following a racing accident.*

I bet Beatrice was in her element researching rocket fuel. It didn't stop there for Beatrice either. Another enterprising adventure was designing a bobsled for the Royal Air Force (RAF) Winter Olympics.

The bobsled was designed and built outside normal working hours at Farnborough, but never made it, mainly due to under funding and the modifications needed to comply with regulations.

Limited testing was undertaken in St Moritz, but it clashed with another major racing event, so never really stood a chance.

Nevertheless, I imagine it was a real whizz on the track! Although Beatrice continued to seek funding to modify and improve the design none was forthcoming, so her dream of a new racing adventure, this time as a spectator never materialised.

Beatrice worked on an earlier RAF bob sled similar to this 1968 model © John Brown

Today, however, I am certain funding would have been available from many sources as the need to win and promote companies worldwide via the Olympics is common place.

It certainly beats our plastic ones used to bump and slide down Butser Hill on the odd occasion when we get enough snow to do so.

Retirement doesn't mean sit back and relax!

Beatrice had fun in her retirement in a variety of ways. You can guess some of them! During it Beatrice carried on providing expertise via consultancy work; was a keen and experienced pistol shot, perhaps originally linked to those younger days cleaning her father's rifles, but also carried on her love of bikes and cars.

She raced around Surrey in her classic Triumph Dolomite Sprint until no longer able to do so. Chronic pain made movement difficult in her later

©inventricity

years. It must have been so frustrating laced with sadness for somebody who had such an active brain and once an energetic and vigorous body that didn't know how to stop, but was forced to do so.

Beatrice also enjoyed reading and watching motor sport on television. Although she didn't compete in the 1967 Grand Prix herself, she had the opportunity to investigate the F1 driver Dan Gurney's engine which had serious mechanical issues. These prevented him from finishing in the race alongside the leading competitors and achieving a successful win.

Occasionally she entertained family members and kept in touch with a few close friends, too. Dennis and Anne (Gladys), her sister, being regular visitors along with social calls from her nieces and nephew. It was good to keep in touch, catch up with family events and discover what David, Janet, Marian and their families were doing.

© DERA Farnborough in Freudenberg: Negative Gravity (2003)

Beatrice looks closely at the Gurney Weslake engine. Mechanical troubles prevented Dan Gurney from finishing among the leaders of the 1967 Grand Prix World Championship. *DERA, Farnborough*

Wretchedly and probably quite painfully, Dr Beatrice Shilling died aged 81 on November 18, 1990 from cancer of the spine.

She smoked like a trooper, but no evidence suggested that cancer affected her lungs, although she had spent years fighting off hacking coughs to no avail. *Don't take up smoking!*

According to Dennis, Beatrice's sister Nora had orthopaedic problems due to osteoporosis, a loss of bone density and strength, resulting in her body *'shrivelling pathetically'*, and sadly dying at 89 in pain, too. His first wife, Anne (Nancie), B's sister, lived until she was 103! Longevity appears to be prevalent for some family members, though sadly not for Beatrice.

This remarkable female engineer, who was born and raised in Waterlooville until five years old, played an instrumental role in defeating the Nazis during the Second World War having invented her 'orifice', a safety device, for the carburettors of Hurricane and Spitfire Merlin engines. This RAE restrictor saved so many lives.

A few years ago, Beatrice was featured in Winchester's Heritage Open Days during September 2018, where she was celebrated as an *'Extraordinary Woman of Hampshire'*. Notable local women from both the past and present were recognised for their achievements.

I do wish I had met her and asked her so many questions about her racing and love of bikes. Maybe I could have been a pillion passenger on her Enfield, Matchless or Norton had I been older or even a co-driver in her racing cars. I dream.

If only time travelling was a reality.

Mind you, I'd have loved to have met my Great Grandfather, too, and discovered more about his love of bikes, cars and his days in the RAF as a '**Brylcreme boy**' during WWII. I think the old family photos need searching for some clues, don't you?

Incidentally, Grandma was very excited this week because she had some very special correspondence – a reply from the RAF to discover her Dad's military records as he had now left this earth twenty five years ago and she is next of kin.

My mind was buzzing with questions. I wondered if he actually flew a plane, or was a passenger being transported to India and Burma. Did he do ground work skittering around on a motor bike?

Was he one of those that flew to support the D-Day evacuation? The only thing she has dropped into our conversations was that he was a Leading Aircraft mechanical engineer working on the Hercules aircraft engines during the war. *No wonder he tinkered with bikes!*

It would appear that both Great Grandad and Beatrice worked towards helping our pilots in WWII!

Great Grandad in his RAF uniform 1944

Beatrice obviously achieving highly with her wonderful brain, hard work and RAE restrictor which was the first stage in solving the fuel problems in Merlin engines fitted to Spitfires and Hurricanes.

I can't wait to find out the rest about my Great Grandad!

Beatrice making history all over again!

Earlier I said Beatrice's birthday would go down in history. Today, International Women's Day (IWD) is celebrated on March 8th - Beatrice's birthday! 2020's campaign theme is;

#EachforEqual

An equal world is an enabled world

It is a day to celebrate female achievements across the world, especially, like Tilly, in what was considered a man's world. IWD aims to seek a more balanced world where both male and females are treated equally.

The idea to promote it as an international event came from Clara Zetkin in 1910. She proposed her notion to one hundred women from seventeen different countries, all of whom, were attending an International Conference of Working Women in Copenhagen. They backed her unanimously and it became an annual event from 1911 in Austria, Denmark, Germany and Switzerland.

In addition the IWD's purpose is to achieve an increased awareness to avoid prejudice as well as improve working and living environments that are much better for all regardless of nationality, gender and birth.

Although only one day a year is allocated to celebrating this, work carries on every day to raise consciousness and action. It is a global campaign with the same themes worldwide. The UK's Suffragette movement is also included but it began ahead of IWD.

The campaign theme for 2021, is;

#Choose To Challenge

IWD believe,

A challenged world is an alert world.

And from challenge comes change.

So choose to challenge!

Beatrice 'Tilly' Shilling would have supported IWD without a doubt. As an early pioneer for women's rights in the workplace, society and life in general, seeking a more balanced approach for women would have been at the forefront in her eyes. *Almost a century later we have still not achieved equality.* Beatrice proved she could excel at what men do and more; not only in the work place but in play, too. She believed everybody had a talent – both male and female – just waiting to be discovered and nurtured. For example, she aided her niece, Janet, to become a teacher by supporting and helping her during training. *Remember, Beatrice was a first class mathematician and her expertise would have been a tremendous help to Janet, along with her other skills.*

There are many women out there setting extremely high standards and showing the world what they can achieve. Equality should be a two-way objective for both males and females. Diversity needs celebrating and shouted loudly from the rooftops.

Beatrice - our local icon and star

Locally, Beatrice's name has been carved in stone to celebrate her achievements. Recently constructed, Beatrice is remembered as a residential development for the over sixties was completed in London Road Waterlooville, and aptly named Shilling Place in her memory.

Since writing began on this book, the local Library in Waterlooville has commemorated Beatrice with a plaque and ceremony to mark her brilliance and relationship to the town. Havant's Lord Mayor led the ceremony.

"Local inventor, engineer and racing driver, Beatrice Shilling OBE, will be commemorated with a plaque at Waterlooville Library. The Mayor of Havant will officiate."

(The News March 8th 2019)

Maybe my book will appear in the teenage section of the library about famous women and inspire others in the same way Beatrice has inspired me, 100 years apart. *I must donate a few copies. What do you think?*

Slightly further afield in Southampton, the 2Time Theatre group at the Nuffield Theatre produced *'Tilly and the Spitfires!'* a play about Beatrice and her accomplishments. *(2timetheatre.weebly.com/)*

Has Beatrice inspired you to become an engineer?

Beatrice's name and achievements are slowly getting out there and it is about time, too. Beatrice was such an inspiration to all females, especially those who enjoy tinkering in engineering, STEM subjects and can perhaps build a career in that field.

Manchester University, where Beatrice originally undertook her degree, now offer a scholarship of £6000 per year in her name. The Beatrice Shilling Scholarship is open to United Kingdom (UK) and European female students that have applied to the School of Electrical and Electronic Engineering at The University of Manchester via the Universities and Colleges Admissions Service. (UCAS) *www.eee.manchester.ac.uk/study/undergraduate/fees-and-funding/*

Coventry University has also recognised the impact Beatrice made by naming their new engineering and computing building after her. The building will be used to highlight STEM subjects – Science, Technology, Engineering and Maths and is currently under construction by Speller Metcalfe at a cost of £27 million. *https://spellermetcalfe.com/project/beatriceshillingbuilding/*

The Royal Holloway University of London (RHUL) has commemorated Beatrice in their STEM funded building aiming to achieve gender equality. It is estimated that it currently reaches out to 30% of their female students. A percentage well above the female average of uptake in electrical engineering.

Professor Hogg, from RHUL, has stated,

"It's a building you want to be in...it's a place where you feel stimulated to be creative."

https://stridetreglown.com/projects/the-beatrice-shilling-building-rhul/

The Beatrice Shilling Science Building, at their Egham campus was officially opened on 27 March 2019 by Professor Dame Ann Dowling, President of the Royal Academy of Engineering.

Incidentally, Beatrice's brother-in-law, Dennis attended the ceremony, too, along with his second wife.

"Jane (my wife now) and I had an interesting time as guests of Royal Holloway, Egham for the official opening of The Beatrice Shilling Building recently."

Apparently the UK is 20,000 short of engineering graduates with fewer women working in this area than anywhere else in Europe. *20,000 short – this is ludicrous.* The idea behind the new building is to provide first class education to students and minimise this shortfall while encouraging more women to become the next generation of electronic engineers and scientists. Innovation and expertise is crucial to train the world-class engineers for the future. We really do need to be able to compete in an international market.

www.royalholloway.ac.uk/about-us/news/royal-holloway-officially-opens-its-new-state-of-the-art-science-building-the-beatrice-shilling-building/

Come on girls, you are the next generation and some of you with an interest in tinkering around should seriously consider a career in this field. I might even join you there. *Perhaps you could be the next Beatrice Shilling! What could you discover or create?*

Have a drink at the Tilly Shilling

Not to be outdone with educational establishments, JD Wetherspoon, a chain of public houses, pubs to you and me, opened a new one in Farnborough during 2011. It was aptly named the Tilly Shilling to pay tribute to Beatrice with Spitfire controls for door handles and other artefacts from the 1930s including a Spitfire blue

print, aircraft-style seats and a propeller on the wall. It was certainly worth a visit for lunch or you could just pop in for a drink and crisps.

Apparently, the nickname 'Tilly' was a bit of an unkind gesture; the name never being used to her face as it was an unflattering reference to her dress sense – that of a rather plain dame.

A Tilly, from the word utility, was a vehicle produced cheaply based on existing car designs during WWII and used by the armed forces at that time.

In wartime, 'tillies' were a low-powered British-made pick-up truck used

© en.wikipedia.org/

by the military such as this Hillman based car for the Navy. Again, a bit of an insult to such an intelligent aeronautical engineer. No man would have been insulted in that manner, which again shows the rather urgent need for gender equality in all walks of life.

Beatrice's memorabilia

Brooklands was Beatrice's favourite track and the world's first purpose-built motor racing circuit so it seems fitting that the Gold Star will now feature in a display at Brooklands Museum, together with the other memorabilia. Andrew Lewis, Museum Curator commented,

"We are delighted to be able to display Beatrice Shilling's badges at the Museum. Her work on the Rolls-Royce Merlin engine which was fitted to many Brooklands built aircraft, combined with being the first of only three women to win a Gold Star makes her a particularly interesting character in Brooklands' history".

https://antique-collecting.co.uk/2015/08/06/beatrices-brooklands-badges-sold/

Beatrice Shilling Timeline

1909: Beatrice was born at 4 Sidney Villas, 236 London Road, Waterlooville, Hampshire to Annie (Nancy) and Henry Shilling on Monday March 8th 1909

1914: The Shilling family moved to Surrey when Beatrice was aged five.

1921: Beatrice and family lived at 65a South Street, Dorking, Surrey. She won the Meccano competition with her moving 'Spinning Wheel' entry in the section for competitors aged between 10 to 14 years of age.

1923: Beatrice bought her first motor cycle an Enfield 2-stroke.

1924: As a teenager Beatrice decided she wanted to be an engineer.

1926: On leaving school Beatrice took up an electrical engineering apprenticeship with Margaret Partridge.

1929: Beatrice borrowed £100 for fees and enrolled on an Electrical Engineering degree in Manchester as one of only two women students. At some point during the next three years Beatrice rode a 1928 Matchless motorbike, racing it in the Peak District as well as a Tandon, a bike produced for the Indian market.

1931: Beatrice shared a room with Muriel Shepherd, a biking friend at Victoria Road, Whalley Range, South Manchester.

1932: She finished her degree (2nd Class) in Electrical Engineering then followed it by undertaking an MSc in Mechanical Engineering.

1933: Beatrice completed her MSc in Mechanical Engineering at Manchester. She began investigating the behaviour of super-charged cylinder engines with Professor Mucklow in Birmingham.

1934: Beatrice started racing at the Brooklands track with a Norton M30 500cc motorcycle, adding a supercharger and lapping the Brooklands track at 106mph. She was awarded the prestigious Brooklands Gold Star for outstanding performances in track and road racing.

1936: The Royal Aircraft Establishment (RAE) in Farnborough employed Beatrice on April 25th as a Technical Author, where she later became a leading specialist in aircraft carburettors.

1938: George and Beatrice wed in Aldershot during September of that year then went to live at Carfield 10 Ashley Road Farnborough.

1940: Beatrice researched and invented the RAE restrictor – Tilly's orifice – to improve fuel problems in Spitfire and Hurricane engines during the Battle of Britain. Although her design reduced the engine stoppages – negative gravity – it did not stop them completely.

1942: She continued, with her team, to improve the design and Rolls-Royce incorporated their final design: the RAE anti-G carburettor, in 1942.

1947: Awarded the OBE for her work during World War II.

1951: An accident, damaging her knee, forced her to give up bike racing.

1955: Beatrice and George moved to Ravenswood Prospect Road Farnborough – it has since been demolished.

1956: Beatrice joined the Institute of Mechanical Engineers as an Associate Member which gave her the qualification of Chartered

Engineer following her promotion at RAE to Senior Principal Scientific Officer (Special Merit) in the Mechanical Engineering Department. *(Part of her application below © Institute of Mechanical Engineers)*

18. Brief details of most important mechanical engineering work for which the candidate has been personally responsible. *The RAE-Wilson injection carburettor was developed initially at the RAE and I was responsible for the design of the prototype carburettor flown in a Wellesley aircraft. This carburettor metered the fuel according to the engine boost pressure and temperature, the r.p.m. and the back pressure. The fuel was injected at the supercharger eye. It was not affected by icing or negative g.*

1962: A serious accident, while motor racing at Goodwood and resulting in the breaking of many bones which also prevented normal circulation, led Beatrice to finish motor racing.

1965: She wrote a summary of her car racing career for the newly formed British Women's Racing Driver's Club. The last entry read:

"23rd June 1962. Members BARC race, Goodwood. Elva Mk VI Sports Racing Car. 1m 48secs in practice. Standing lap in 1m 50 CRASHED. Car written off, driver nearly."

(www.bwrdc.co.uk)   *Car parts of the Elva and others at Carfield ©Roger Dunbar*

1969: Beatrice retired from full time employment at the RAE but still continued with consultancy work there and elsewhere. She also received her Honorary Doctorate at Surrey University in December 1969.

1990: Beatrice died from spinal cancer but was survived by George who lived for a further six years.

Aeronautical engineer Beatrice 'Tilly' Shilling, at the Royal Aeronautical Establishment at Farnborough in The Petersfield Post (2018)

Beatrice Shilling (Naylor)

OBE PhD MSc CEng

1909 – 1990

doing what she loved!

Riding her 197cc Tandon in a post-war Southern Centre trial during the 1930s.
© Sam Hewitt in www.classicmotorcycle.co.uk/beatrice-shilling/

You can do it – did Jessica succeed?

One day, in the not too distant future, maybe a decade away, I hope to make my mark on the world. I may not be a Beatrice Shilling succeeding in the field of aeronautical engineering, but I have started, amongst other things, by successfully learning to ride my unicycle and actually appeared on **This Time Next Year** with Davina McCall to prove it! *(May 2017/8) My secret was out!*

Thanks to Siobhan for having the patience and expertise to teach me and all those church halls that permitted me to topple, crash and eventually slither around seamlessly on one wheel. I hope I don't owe you a pot of paint each to touch up any possible scratches.

Davina and Jessica © GV 2017 (1st filming TTNY)

Getting ready to film for TTNY was so exciting that I still get goose bumps thinking about my experiences. However, lots of exhausting training steered me in that direction.

Nothing comes easily. Determination, enormous amounts of energy and hard work along with an *"I can do it"* attitude is essential to succeed.

A Norton next!

Preparing for filming © GV 2018
(2nd filming TTNY)

Believe in yourself and your dreams might just come true...

Unicycling on TTNY! © GV 2018
(2nd filming TTNY)

Radio Wandsworth

The radio station provided opportunities to broadcast live. At one stage, I had a weekly spot on Fayon Dixon's show, *"The Kids Are Alright"* hosting the Book Quiz. My task was to ask children questions about favourite books and their characters.

It also launched my song, *'Wish'* which I have written and performed about learning to ride my unicycle. The charity single is emphasising the need to persevere and never give up on your dreams. *Build on those first steps! Determination wins!*

I wanted to encourage others to be successful, too. It is available on Amazon Music *(www.amazon.com/Wish-Jessica-Emily-Venn/)* and all profits go to four charities:

Action Medical Research for Children

(https://action.org.uk/   Davina McCall)

Portsmouth Downs Syndrome Association

(https://www.downs-syndrome.org.uk/   Emma Barton East Enders)

Salisbury District Hospital

(www.salisbury.nhs.uk/wards-departments/charities/bugs/fundraising/ where Bertie was treated a few years ago) and

Follow Your Dreams. *(www.followyourdreams.org.uk/— I have a few disabled friends who need support and FYDs do that.)*

Mum just checked the number of streams of my song to date!

I am blessed to be able to follow my dreams, so I hope others can follow their aspirations, too.

What else am I doing?

Last year, I was fortunate to appear in Photobox's shoot to advertise their products for Mother's day 2019 – a paid job – on the Internet. I'll tell you about a few more, but I can't list them all.

© Photobox 2019

In addition, I played the lead in the trailer for **Peace in Our Time**, a movie in the making about the children in World War II who remained at home and did not get evacuated. Please see Mum's photograph of me on set.

© *GV*

Learning British Sign Language (BSL) for an amateur, student movie I am taking the lead in is another challenge for me. I also love computing. Grandma and Mum are members of **Computing at Schools (CAS),** so both have the expertise to help me. So does Dad!

I have several other projects underway including continuing my sailing lessons to obtain Royal Yachting Associations (RYA) level 2. No yacht racing as yet, but ...*life is for living!*

In addition, I was delighted to skateboard for a British Red Cross video on First Aid.

More recently I was fortunate to act in the Unicorn My Fairy Garden television and internet advert. Please watch the video on You Tube at *www.youtube.com/watch?v=KwikXmuUUQM ©Unicorn Fairy Garden*

Travelling on the Portsmouth to Waterloo line last year Dad had a phone call from Blue Peter. Apparently, my application for the new Ed Sheeran Music badge, *'BREAK THE NOISE'* was the first one to be opened and therefore the first in the UK to be awarded it! I am totally chuffed.

Thanks, Grandma for sending it *First Class and Signed For* – I think it made it stand out amongst the hundreds they receive each

week – and that's not all, either!

As requested, Mum e-mailed them some more photos of me playing instruments as the producer wanted to use my application and photo to advertise the badge. Lindsay mentioned me on the show, whilst pointing out a photograph of my first attempt at playing an Australian didgeridoo!

To date, I have FIVE Blue Peter badges including the coveted Diamond badge, but I am aiming to get them all one day! Blue Peter is something I'd love to present when older, so I'll tuck that aspiration away for later, but will need to be very well educated beforehand.

A few years ago I was very privileged to have a dance class taken by Dame Darcey Bussell DBE as well as chat with her at the end of the lesson. Hopefully, my East Enders workshop with Jacqueline Jossa last summer will provide me with some additional expertise for more television work, but imminently I need to concentrate on my 11 plus education, so am off to view another school and meet the Head.

While we're on the subject of schools, I was later awarded a scholarship to that independent school which specialises in the creative arts. Sadly, due to Covid-19 and unsurmountable problems with transport I was unable to take up that amazing opportunity. However, my new school focusses on dance and drama, too. It is also deemed an Outstanding school by OFSTED, so I am not complaining.

Due for release in March 2021 is the supernatural chiller movie, 'The Heiress', in which I play a leading role as Abigail. Awarded an 18 by the film board, I cannot attend the premier or view it. All my takes were filmed independently of the scary stuff.

Another thing I have to wait for, along with my Norton bike!

Learning to play the drums is my latest venture. Watch out for me, please, as Grandma says,

"You can do anything or be anyone you want – just try!"

Checkout my Spotlight credits – it tells you so much more about what I have done and shows what *you* could achieve, too.

Remember it all starts with your first steps and hard work.

NEVER GIVE UP!

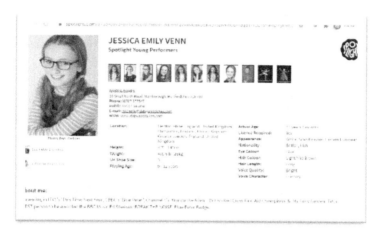

https;//www.spotlight.com/9735-8973-6410

Life is hectic, challenging and exhausting at times, but I love it!

NEWS FLASH! Only last week my latest success was this Musical Theatre Singing exam in which I scored 96% – even I am amazed by the results!

What can you do?

Don't be modest, celebrate your achievements and go out for what you want in life. Beat or at least equalise with the boys in your ambitions! There is plenty of talk on the web about including women and minority groups in having equal opportunities, but it is not happening fast enough. The IWD website states,

"Gender parity will not be attained for almost a century. There's urgent work to do – and we can all play a part." (2020)

The technology industry is amongst the poorest for diversity and equal opportunities when it comes to selecting women in senior posts never mind on their boards of directors. Sadly, gender issues reign.

"I raise my voice, not so I can shout, but so that those without a voice can be heard. We cannot succeed, when half of us are held back." Malala Yousafzia (2016)

We need to change that; whether you are male or female, like Beatrice, influence the powers that control our workplaces and schools. *STEM for all! Equality for all!*

* *Show them your skills*

* *Celebrate diversity*

* *Be proud of yourself!*

* **YOU CAN DO IT!**

Guess who I met at the hairdressers? **Emma Barton** is a local girl who has worked hard, shown determination and now stars in East Enders! *She did it, so can you!* Did you see her on Strictly Come Dancing?

Please read *Beatrice & Jessica This Girl Can* to find out a lot more about what I have undertaken along with Beatrice's story. Perhaps it will give you some ideas to make your dreams come true. *It may only be a tiny objective, but it could mean the world to you. Try it!*

Glossary: including those terms known by their abbreviated form

*Ada Lovelace – the daughter of Lord Bryon, a famous poet, was a talented mathematician and is said to have written instructions – algorithms – for Charles Babbage's Different and Analytical Engines: early calculators and computers in the 1800s.

*Ambidextrous – means being able to use both hands equally well to write, draw and manipulate objects, usually with skill.

*Aeronautical engineer(s) – would undertake work on the different components that make up aircraft and their systems e.g. fuel or propulsion etc. Environmental issues are of grave concern and increasingly requires expertise is reducing the impact of flight pollution. More recently the term used would be an aerospace engineer, working on planes or space craft.

*Babbage Charles – was born in 1791 and was fascinated by maths from an early age. He taught himself algebra and used his skills to explore technology and his *'computer systems'* of that time; the most famous being his Difference Engine to calculate tables followed by the Analytical Engine, a fore runner of computers. Due to lack of funding it was never completed.

*Battle of Britain in 1940 – Hitler wanted to invade Britain hoping Churchill would agree a peace arrangement, but that did not happen. The battle was mainly airborne across the south coast of England during the summer and autumn of 1940.

The RAF ensured the Germans did not gain control of our air space. Although it did not finish the war it helped considerably in preparing for Operation Overlord, the 1944 battle in Normandy to overcome the Germans occupation in Western Europe and end the war.

*BSA (Birmingham Small Arms Company Limited) – was a group of British industrialists who manufactured a whole range of products including firearms for both leisure and the military. In addition they created bicycles, motorcycles, cars, buses and tools of many descriptions.

*BRIO – a wonderful wooden based toy which was first made in Sweden by a family firm of carpenters in 1884. It comprises of a whole host of toys that fit together to create towns and villages with railway tracks, houses, animals, vehicles, bridges, cranes with magnets, boats and lots more. It encourages children to use their imagination during play; improve language skills, dexterity and explore trial and error while attempting to make the train track fit together or build bridges that stay up. Ours is 37 years old, looks brand new and is the most robust *'adventure'* in the toy cupboard! *A wonderful early STEM toy.*

*Brylcreem – During WWII thousands of young men joined the RAF. Many were from middle class homes, who always took pride in their appearances. Brylcreem used this as a marketing ploy, so employed Airmen in their adverts. Consequently, the RAF males became known as Brylcreem Boys which started a popular trend and increased their sales. To improve their looks and style they used Brylcreem, a greasy alternative to today's wax.

*Computing at Schools (CAS) – Computing is our future; so every child needs the best teaching and first-hand experience it can receive to ensure they are ready for today and what is to come. CAS is an organisation incorporating teachers, university staff, IT experts and developers as well as other professionals and parents to support and equip schools to promote and make certain their passion for first class computer education happens. They hold local meetings in schools and universities where members share their expertise, often by practical means and first-hand experience. This can then be cascaded to staff and pupils within schools and at home.

*Daisy the Dinosaur – is a free app to help young children learn basic coding through animation. They can drag and drop the blocks of scripts to make daisy jump, spin, and move forward as well as backwards on the screen. The Challenge options increase the skills level and introduces sequencing and loops in more detail. Solving the app's challenges helps this but reading the instructions is increasingly more difficult for pre-school children. However, with support they soon learn to read the script blocks and challenges unaided. Made by Hopscotch.

App Store: https://hop.sc/get_hopscotch
Website: https://www.gethopscotch.com

*Driver and Vehicle Licensing Agency (DVLA) – is based in Swansea, Wales. It holds over 48 million drivers' records and 40 million records of vehicles, including motorbikes, lorries and cars etc. on its database. In addition it collects the road tax due on vehicles. Specialist number plates, such as those with unusual registrations can be purchased here.

People who have not paid the due tax are followed up and can be fined if caught. In addition it deals with medical issues for drivers to ensure they are safe to drive. The staff also record and mark up licences with penalty points etc. should a driver have committed an offence such as speeding. Another duty is to assist the police in any crime related issues involving drivers or vehicles such as accidents or thefts.

*Grace Hopper – was a USA computer scientist who worked on the Harvard Mark 1 computer. She was a Rear Admiral in the Navy and helped decode enemy messages. In addition she was a maths professor and wrote some of the first code for computers leading to COBOL; standing for COmmon Business Oriented Language.

*LegoWeDo2 – creates opportunities to combine science, technology and computing skills in an enjoyable way to make working Lego models. Using code on a tablet or similar device and following web-based instructions to create a moving, script-controlled model, children can explore trial and error; check out solutions and explore scientific options which develop their problem solving expertise in a fun way. It provides hands-on experience, as well as aiding computational thinking skills through asking scientific and computer based questions linked to their experimentation.
https://education.lego.com/en-gb/ & *https://education.lego.com/en-gb/homeschool*

*Meccano – Frank Hornby, manufacturer of the famous trains invented Meccano around 1898. It was a construction kit of metal strips, nuts, bolts, plates, wheels, axles, angled girders and gears to build working models. It is still much sought after today but it is now mainly manufactured from plastic rather than tin plate.

*MOT** – The Ministry of Transport (as it was) test checks that your vehicle meets road safety and environmental standards. It is essential once a car is three years old and must be tested and pass every year before legally being allowed on the road.

*Motor Car Act of 1903** – was introduced by Parliament to increase speed limits from 14 to 20mph as well as vehicle registration which required each vehicle to show number plates. Drivers paid five shillings to obtain a licence, although no test was required. Any reckless driving resulted in a court appearances and a fine.

*Negative g** – Gravity is a force of attraction that exists between any two masses anywhere in the universe. The bigger the object, the greater the gravity – so the Earth's is greater than the moon's. We say that the Earth's standard form of gravity is 1G, equivalent to travelling at 9.8 meters per second. **G-force** is a force created by something travelling at a speed of more than 9.8 meters per second and can act against gravity. An example would be travelling on a rollercoaster.

Negative G-force is when something accelerates downwards with the pull of gravity. In early Spitfires, fighting manoeuvres caused a rapid change from positive to negative G forces which stopped the carburettor functioning properly. There was either too much or too little fuel, so sometimes the planes crashed. Positive G-force is when something accelerates upwards against the pull of gravity.

*Norton Commando** – a British built motorbike that is attractive and holds the road well. Although very expensive compared to Japanese bikes, it does not have unnecessary devices and additions.

*Norton Manx 500 – is a British racing motorbike built between 1947 and 1962. There has been a Norton in every Isle of Man TT race since it started in 1907 through to the 1970s. You can still purchase a Manx as it is sought after worldwide. Nortons have an enormous fan base. *Jessica is seated on a 1957 Manx on the back cover of this book. She also had a go on an older model from 1947 – one of the first ever made!*

*Peace in Our Time – the story of children who remained at home during WWII rather than be evacuated to the countryside for safety. The trailer can be watched at *www.youtube.com/watch?v=QBEtVG1eBsE*

*PhotoBox – produce photo books, cards, mugs, wall art and lots more from electronic photos. www.photobox.co.uk/

*Podcast – an audio/sound file that can be downloaded or uploaded to the internet.

*Professor Mucklow – was appointed assistant lecturer in engineering at Manchester University in 1922, and in 1926 later became a lecturer. By 1940 he was selected as Chance Professor of Mechanical Engineering at Birmingham University, one of his interests being the carburettor. *Beatrice worked with him.* Currently, Birmingham University offer a prize in his name for the best submitted project in the final year of the Bachelor of Engineering programme.

*Radio Wandsworth – was a local London-based radio station. *It has now been rebranded as Riverside Radio. www.riversideradio.com/*

*Royal Aircraft Establishment (RAE) – was a British research centre based in Farnborough, Hampshire specialising in aircraft. Much scientific and mechanical work on all sorts of aircraft and components etc. has been carried out here, especially during WWII. Experts are also set the task of establishing why aircraft failed or sustained accidents. At one point the Ministry of Defence (MOD) was responsible for it. However in more recent times it is was known as the Royal Aerospace Establishment and now forms part of the Defence Research Agency.

*Royal Enfield – Based in Redditch, Worcestershire. The Enfield Cycle Company made motor cycles, bicycles, lawnmowers and engines. Originally they made weapons as their logo shows a cannon with the moto *"Made like a gun"*. Their brand name Royal Enfield was licensed by the Crown in 1890. Currently the bikes are made in Chennai, India. *www.royalenfield-uk.co.uk/history*

*Sir Lancelot du Lac – was it a fairy tale, Celtic legend or really true? It was said that Lancelot was the son of King Ban of Benwick and Queen Elaine. He was also the first knight of King Arthur's Round Table and the greatest fighter of all the knights. Although it may well be a myth, throughout the centuries King Arthur, Guinevere and Lancelot have held our interest via movies and stories and will do so for many more years to come.

*Site of Special Scientific Interest – is an area of protected land or water as defined by the European Union's Habitats Directive because it contains unique species or habitats of high scientific value for conservation. Rules are in place to register and protect such land and species.

*STEM – Science, Technology, Engineering and Maths, subjects taught at school, clubs and further education colleges to encourage an early interest in developing the WOW factor of STEM.

The aim is to promote future careers enabling the UK to have a strong position in world markets through links with industry. The arts have been added in some cases, so now we have STEAM.

*Stemettes – is an organisation that engages first-hand to inspire young girls from 5 upwards with technology, maths, science and engineering (STEM). The purpose is to encourage them to change the world's attitude to become more gender neutral by increasing the number of females in these subjects. The girls hold events all over the country in schools, clubs and halls. Dr. Anne-Marie Imafidon's team's expertise taught us how to legally *'hack'* websites such as the BBC by overlaying a *'false homepage'* through coding. It was fun!

*Stickle Bricks – Are an early construction/technology toy for toddlers to help dexterity as well as imagination. They are brightly coloured plastic bricks that lock together in any formation children want. The *'people heads'* are great for pilots, mums and dads, pre-school friends – whatever they think up! The bricks can be pulled apart and used repeatedly. Denys Fisher invented it in 1969.

*This Time Next Year – was a television programme hosted by Davina McCall. The aim of the programme, set over a year, encourages children and adults, able bodied as well as disabled, to make a pledge on television to do something within the next year. A year later, those that have made a pledge are brought back and filmed again to celebrate their successes. Technology enables both sets of films to be shown simultaneously. Not all participants are shown on TV. It depends on the slots available and how well it seamlessly fits together for the show. Jessica was fortunate to be selected for the programme, but only for a short time – enough to demonstrate that she had succeeded in riding her unicycle. The programme ceased to be broadcast in 2020.

*Universities and Colleges Admission Service (UCAS) – is used by students to apply for an undergraduate university place in the UK.

*VLE – a virtual learning environment is an accessible website but enclosed within a safe environment, particularly for schools. Members will have a user name and password, allowing it to be accessed from home and school. Within it, you usually have your own private web page and access to e-mail, Wikis, blogs and forums to discuss whatever is relevant at that time. Photos, text and images from websites as well as your own can be inserted, but be aware of copyright © and reference it if not your own material. Schools often add homework, information about the curriculum and meetings to their VLE and websites. Putting up fun work to do on snow days was always a popular choice to avoid boredom!

*V Tech-Flight scheme – A scheme set up at the Royal Aircraft Establishment to enable competent aircraft staff to learn how to fly aircraft.

*Wikis – The important part of a wiki, as in Wikipedia, is that many users can get together to add and edit information online. In schools a wiki may be set up by a teacher on a particular subject and children add their ideas, information and images to it, again often on a VLE to ensure safety and security.

*Women's Engineering Society – The organisation celebrated its centenary in June 2019. When established in 1919 it was intended to improve equality for women in engineering, especially during the war years. When men returned from war many women returned to the kitchen. The men re-established their roles in the work force. 100 years later only about 12% of the engineering work force are women.

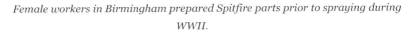

Female workers in Birmingham prepared Spitfire parts prior to spraying during WWII.

© *www.birminghammail.co.uk/news/midlands-news/how-saucepans-built-spitfires-won-8892852*

In a remarkable event, to raise funds to build the planes, some housewives donated their metal saucepans! A 1940 fund collected over £4,000, including £75 raised by children from a local primary school. Women undertook all kinds of work when the men were called up or volunteered to join the forces and fight.

Bibliography:

Alan (2018) Alan's Meccano: *Image of old Meccano 1911-12*
    Available from: www.alansmeccano.org (Accessed: March
    2018 & January 2019)

Austin Healey Sprite (2020) *Image of a similar car to Beatrice's*
    Available from: www.sportscar2.com (Accessed: Sept 2020)

BBC (2017) *Beatrice Shilling: Pioneering engineer's genius 'helped
    win World War Two'* Available from: www.bbc.co.uk/news/
    uk-england-manchester-40267364 (Accessed: Dec 2018)

BBC (2020) IWD 2020 *—History, strikes and celebrations: When
    did it all start? Clara Zetkin* Available from:
    www.bbc.co.uk/news/world (Accessed: November 2020)

BBC (2019) *Blue Peter Music Badge/Ed Sheeran* Available from:
    www.bbc.co.uk/cbbc/joinin/bp-music-badge
    (Accessed: 2019)

BBC (2017) *Brooklands racetrack finishing straight re-opened*
    Available from: www.bbc.co.uk/news/uk-england-surrey-
    40314868 (Accessed: Sept 2020)

Birmingham Mail *(2015) How saucepans built Spitfires* Available
    from: www.birminghammail.co.uk/news/midlands-
    news/how-saucepans-built-spitfires-won (Accessed: 2018)

Bisley (2018) *Bisley Shooting Range* Available from:
    www.bisleyshooting.co.uk/ (Accessed: 2018)

Blake-Coleman Barrie (2016) *The Fabulous Tilly Shilling* Available
    from: www.inventricity.com/tilly-shilling (Accessed: 2019)

British Women's Racing Driver's Club (2018) *Members BARC race Beatrice Shilling* Available from: www.bwrdc.co.uk (Accessed: 2018)

Brooklands (1939) *Last Race at Brooklands* Available from: www.brooklandsmuseum.com/explore/our-history/motor-racing (Accessed: December 2018)

Brooklands (c1930s) Poster – *Racing at Brooklands* Available from: www.brooklandsmuseum.com/explore/our-history/motor-racing (Accessed: December 2018)

Brown John (1968) *RAF Bobsleigh Team* Available from: www.hjcbrown.com/olympic-bobsleigh-team-1968.htm (Accessed: September 2019)

BSA: (2018) *BSA Motorcycles* Available from: https://en.wikipedia.org/wiki/BSAmotorcycles (Accessed: February 2019)

BSA ZB315 (1962) *Motor Cycle Service Invoice from Chambers Belfast* Available from: Personal Family History Documents (Accessed: September 2020)

Cameron Edward (1910) *The importance of a carburetor* in the New York Times Available from: www.nytimes.com/1910/10/16/archives/importance-of-carburetor-function-performed-to-properly-control-the.html (Accessed: February 2019)

Census of England and Wales (1911) *Residents of Sidney House (aka 4 Sidney Villas) the Shilling family and servants* Available from: www.ancestry.co.uk (Accessed: March 2019)

Channel 4 (2020) *Inside the Spitfire Factory* Available from: www.channel4.com/programmes/inside-the-spitfire-factory/on-demand/70073-005 (Accessed: 27.10.20)

Computing at School (CAS) (2008) *Our Purpose and Mission* Available from: www.computingatschool.org.uk/about (Accessed: 2014 & January 2019)

Coventry University (2019) *Beatrice Shilling Building* Available from: www.spellermetcalfe.com/project/beatriceshillingbuilding (Accessed: January 2019)

Cryer AB (2018) *Beatrice Shilling Explained* Available from: https://everything.explained.today/Beatrice_Shilling/ (Accessed: December 2018)

Dunbar Roger (2006) *Elva Jottings* Available from: www.elva.com/history/aug06-jottings02.html (Accessed: December 2018)

Farnborough Society (2020) *Beatrice Shilling Plaque* Available from: https://thefarnboroughsociety.org.uk/ (Accessed: October 2020 online and via Contact Form)

Francis Frith (2019) *Waterlooville The Village 1906 (e-card photo)* Available from: www.francisfrith.com (*licence purchased 16.4.19*) (Accessed: April 2019)

Freudenberg Matthew (2003) *Negative Gravity: A life of Beatrice Shilling (Lagonda image p119, George Naylor p74, Beatrice pp 12, 29, Letters pp 59, 60 & 66, F1 car 121.* © *Dennis Lock* Charlton Press: UK

Gandhi Mahatma (2020) *Diversity Quotes* Available from:
www.wisesayings.com/diversity-quotes
(Accessed December 2020)

Gordano (2016) *Miss Shillings Orifice image* Available from:
https://gordanohomefront.wordpress.com/2016/02/11/mis
s-shillings-orifice/ (Accessed: March 2019)

Grand Prix (2109) *Lella Lombardie* Available from:
www.grandprix.com/gpe/drv-lomlel.html
(Accessed: April 2019)

Harley-Davidson (2018) *Harley-Davidson Motorbikes*
Available from: www.harley-davidson.com
(Accessed: March 2018 & January 2019)

Hewitt Sam (2018) *Beatrice Shilling* Available from:
https://www.classicmotorcycle.co.uk/beatrice-shilling/
(Accessed: 2018)

Holloway James (2020) *How-miss-shillings-orifice-helped-win-
the-war/* Available from:www.damninteresting.com/
(Accessed: November 2020)

Hopper Grace (2020) *Computer Scientist & Rear Admiral*
Available from: Wikipedia Foundation
https://en.wikipedia.org/wiki/Grace_Hopper
(Accessed: 2018 and 2020)

Institution of Mechanical Engineers (2020) *IWD 2020 Highlight
on Beatrice* Shilling *Available from: IME
https://imechearchive.wordpress.com* (Accessed: 2020)

International Unicycle Federation (2019) *Skills* Available from: https://unicycling.org/ (Accessed: 2019)

International Women's Day (2019/20) /*#EachforEqual 2020 #ChooseToChallenge 2021* Available from: www.internationalwomensday.com (Accessed: January 2019 & November 2020)

LAT Photographic Archive (1957) in Matthew Freudenberg (2003) *Negative Gravity A life of Beatrice Shilling* p 119 Charlton Publications: UK (Accessed: November 2020)

Lego (2017) *LegoWeDo2* Available from: https://education.lego.com/ (Accessed: Autumn 2017) LEGO Lockdown support @ https://education.lego.com/en-gb/homeschool *(2021)*

Lewis Andrew (2019) *Beatrice's memorabilia and badges* Available from: https;//antique-collecting.co.uk/2015/08/06/beatrices-brooklands-badges-sold/ (Accessed: January 2019)

Locke Dennis & Woodford David (1910 – 1980) *Beatrice Shilling and family photographs* Available from: Dennis Locke *(brother-in-law)* and David Woodford *(nephew)* (Accessed: 2019 – 2020)

Lovelace Ada (2018) *Ada Lovelace* Available from: Wikipedia Foundation https://enWikipedia.org/wiki/adalovelace (Accessed: 2018 – 2020)

McCarthy & Stone (2019) *Beatrice Shilling Building* Available from www.mccarthyandstone.co.uk/retirement-properties-for-sale/shilling-place/ (Accessed: March 2019)

McKay Feargal (2017) *the Giro d'Italia Alfonsina Strada* Available from: www.podiumcafe.com/book-corner/ (Accessed: 2018)

Matchless (2020) *Matchless Motorcycles* Available from: www.classic-british-motorcycles.com/matchless-motorcycles.html & www.matchlesslondon.com/blog (Accessed: November 2020)

Manchester University (2019) *Beatrice Shilling Scholarship* Available from: www.eee.manchester.ac.uk/study/undergraduate/fees-and-funding/ (Accessed: January 2019)

Manchester University (2015) *Beatrice Shilling – Engineer and Battle of Britain Heroine* Available from: https://www.manchester.ac.uk/discover/news/beatrice-shilling--engineer-and-battle-of-britain-heroine/ (Accessed: November 2018)

Marriott Roger (2020) *Meccano Magazine article on Beatrice winning a competition.* Available by e-mail & www.nzmeccano.com July/August 1921 (Accessed: November 2020)

Marshallsay JJ (2020) *Horndean Light Railway in Memories of Bygone Portsmouth* Available from: Facebook www.facebook.com/groups/366005550201426 (Accessed: November 2020)

Norton (2018) *Norton Commando* Available from: www.nortonmotorcycles.com (Accessed: January 2019)

Newman Cathy (2018) *Bloody Brilliant Women: The Pioneers, Revolutionaries and Geniuses Your History Teacher Forgot to Mention* London: Collins

Nuffield Theatre Southampton (2019) *Tilly and the Spitfires* (Showing Feb 2019) Available from: nstheatres.co.uk (Accessed: January 2019)

Petersfield Post (2018) *Nostalgia: Hampshire has been at the heart of military history* Available from: www.petersfieldpost.co.uk (Accessed: November 2018).

Professor Mucklow (1954) *Institution of Mechanical Engineers in* Grace's Guide to British History. Available from: www.gracesguide.co.uk (Accessed: January 2019)

Red Cross (2018) *First Aid Training for Children* Available from: https://firstaidchampions.redcross.org.uk/primary/ (Accessed: May 2019)

Reese Peter (2019) *Merlin Engine image 1942* Available from: www.thehistorypress.co.uk/articles/beatrice-tilly-shilling-celebrated-aeronautical-and-motorcycle-engineer (Accessed 2019 and 2020)

Richard (2020) *Image of Royal Enfield bike* Available from: www.facebook.com/RedDevilMotors (Accessed: Sept.2020)

Royal Holloway London University (2019) *The Beatrice Shilling Building named in her memory* Available from: https://stridetreglown.com/projects/the-beatrice-shilling-building-rhul/ (Accessed: January 2019)

Seth (2017) *Learn to ride a unicycle: Seth's bike hacks* Available from: www.youtube.com/watch?v=6NT8upwdMQo (Accessed: December 2017 and January 2019)

Shilling Beatrice (2018) *Beatrice Shilling* Available from: Wikipedia Foundation en.wikipedia.org/wiki/Beatrice Shilling (Accessed: November 2018)

Surrey University (2017) *IWD Beatrice Shilling: Honorary PhD* Available from: https://blogs.surrey.ac.uk/archives/2017/03/08/internatio nal-womens-day-the-inspirational-beatrice-shilling-2/ (Accessed: 2019)

The News (2019) *Local inventor, engineer and racing driver, Beatrice Shilling OBE Celebrated* Available in The News March 8th 2019 (Accessed: March 2019)

Unicorn (2019) *Unicorn My Fairy Garden (television and internet advert).* Available from: www.youtube.com/watch?v=Kwik XmuUUQM_(Accessed: 2020)

Venn G (2018) *Jessica unicycle, skateboard & other images TTNY, Home & Southsea (2018 - 2020)* Available from: Personal family photos. (Accessed: 2017, 2018, 2019 & 2020)

Waterlooville Library Staff (2019) *Commemoration Beatrice Shilling in Havant Council News* Available from: www.havant.gov.uk/ Staff provided Information including:

Nottingham Journal (Monday 01 November 1937, page 3)

Meccano competition (1921) *Portsmouth News (1938) Beatrice Shilling's Racing Win.* (Accessed: March 2019)

Wetherspoon JD Pubs (2018) *The Tilly Shilling in Farnborough* Available from: www.jdwetherspoon.com (Accessed: 2018)

Winchester Heritage (2018) *Extraordinary Women of Hampshire exhibition: Beatrice Shilling* Available from: www.winchesterheritageopendays.org/blog/2018/9/17/extraordinary-women-of-hampshire (Accessed: March 2019)

Yousafazia Malala (2016) 11 *Inspiring gender equality quotes that will leave you thinking* Available from: www.womensweb.in/2016/06/ (Accessed: January 2021)

Acknowledgements:

David Woodford, Beatrice's nephew for providing the early photographs of the Shilling girls – much appreciated - along with some snippets about Beatrice that I was unaware of including her skills in being ambidextrous and her house named Carfield! Also for keeping in touch over the writing of this book. *I enjoy our e-mails.*

Dennis Lock, Beatrice's brother-in-law, for providing background information on George, Beatrice and her sisters Nora and Nancy as well as B's parents, her nieces, Janet and Marion and nephew David. Such kind words about his mother-in-law, Annie, who sounds a real gem – if only we all could have such a sweet mother-in-law! Thanks for permission to use the photographs etc., too. *What a treasure trove you have!*

Eric Jackson's family, especially Steve and his Mum, who provided information about the shop in the early days, but sadly only had family holiday snaps and nothing on Sidney Villas in the 1900s. Eric was a founder member of the Waterlooville Motorcycle Club along with the Rev. Bruce Cornford in 1928. *Beatrice was a biker then, too!*

Geoff and Roger for trailering their Norton Manx bikes to the Forest of Bere pub for the photo shoot regardless of the weather that day. *You are both amazing! Thanks for the follow up chat, too, Geoff.*

Joan Foster for providing details about her niece, Judy Derisley, Beatrice's God-daughter; also *'Carfield'* and its concrete floor! *The confirmation was good to have.*

Peter Hurst from the TFS for your prompt contacting skills via The Farnborough Society (TFS) in forwarding my request to Joan in the first instance. *It is much appreciated, thank you.*

John Brooks from the Solent branch of the Norton Owners Club (NOC) for arranging a photo shoot with two rather elderly Manx bikes, their owners and Jessica. *Wet but wonderful, thanks.*

Judy Derisley God-daughter of Beatrice. Comments available via The Spitfire Factory Ch4 *I have written to Judy for further details but as yet have not received a reply.*

Trish Earle and the Denmead Book Club for reading and commenting on my first draft – such sound suggestions, thank you! *I have added a little more about Jessica as requested.*

Verity, from Waterlooville Library for her help in tracking down information on Beatrice and supplying the article from the Nottingham Journal etc. as well as the information about the Meccano competition. *Thank you so much for reading part of my first draft and encouraging me to continue with the book.*

Wendy Freudenberg, the wife of the late Matthew Freudenberg, for her chatty e-mails and information about her inspiring grandchildren – *one a male ballet dancer* – but also for putting me in touch with Beatrice's family. *An amazing feat!*

My Family - including my husband for his undying support including reading and re-reading my drafts; Gemma & Ian for their detailed texts on everything unicycling and TTNY. Bertie, my cuddly and funny plane and racing car buddy; J my son for the crates of old Dinky cars he gave me for Bertie to keep him occupied, further develop his interest in vehicles and ask endless questions about them. Lastly, to the lovely and talented Jessica who provided the inspiration to link Beatrice's story with hers. *One day you will make your mark, even more so than in the last decade!*

Richard & Ali Inskip for providing the setting at the Forest of Bere (FOB) for the NOC photo shoot – pity about the rain! The FOB hosts the meetings for the NOC in non-Covid times, as well as Denmead Book Club. *Great hosts at all times!*

BOOKS BY ELSIE O'NEILL

TRADITIONAL SKIPPING SONGS WITH JESSICA & GRANDMA

Jessica & Grandma have collaborated well during Lockdown to produce this superb skipping book. There are 80 plus traditional rhymes to involve children and adults of all ages in exercise and physical activities at home, in the playground or for PE at school. It encourages pupils to learn the rhymes whilst performing physical activity either individually or in pairs/groups.

The rhymes have great cross curricular links to history, English, geography and various cultural influences from not only the UK but other countries around the world.

The rhymes and exercises could be used either as a warm up/cool down or as part of a main lesson, too, in both primary and secondary schools.

The You Tube channel with demonstrations is a fabulous added extra to support the teaching of the skipping steps and songs – a great idea. I will certainly be using it to teach my class of future Olympic winning skippers! A great warm-up prior to football and rugby for all ages.

A brilliant resource for teachers, coaches and parents!

OFSTED WILL LOVE SEEING IT IN ACTION! *(EV)*

The book has also been used in care/nursing homes to encourage the patients to relive their youth by singing the songs and recalling childhood memories – music helps here! Conversations are flowing, laughter is explosive, spontaneous and so natural; all skipping along nicely! In addition to PE schools are using it with the lunchtime supervisors to teach skipping and the accompanying songs. The children are enjoying it, knowing granny skipped along to some of them which encourages conversations with grandparents and other family members.

Available from Amazon.

Read the e-book for free if a Kindle member.

BEATRICE & JESSICA – THIS GIRL CAN is a much more detailed version about both females, STEaM and how it is being tackled in schools etc. as well as the urgent need for a more gender balanced world. It is currently on hold while waiting for permission to use a few images, but will be available on Amazon in 2021.

GRANDMA'S DNA & OTHER STUFF

Jessica and Grandma have set out to discover more about their family history. In doing so, they investigate Grandma's DNA and gain quite a bit of knowledge about it, too.

Can you even say deoxyribonucleic acid? DNA is easier!

Was Grandma related to a Viking warrior who set sail for Scotland in a longboat prior to arriving in Ireland?

Is there a clue hiding in her brother's 'Viking finger' which requires amputation? Maybe yes, maybe no; but who knows.

Perhaps she was a distant relative of Boudicca and the Iceni tribe? *Look at that hair!*

What has Africa got to do with any of it? *She is Irish!*

Grandma is certainly of Celtic origins, but there is more to her than her long, curly red hair and determined feminist nature which ensures equality for all that follow in her wake.

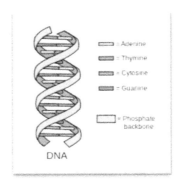

COMING SOON TO AMAZON!

Watch out for JESSICA'S COOK BOOK in 2021.

Try her recipe for Great, Great Granny's sponge cake.

ABOUT THE AUTHOR

I grew up in Belfast during the 1950s and 1960s. There were six children in total, the youngest being 19 years younger than me. (Viking finger man!)

We played in the street, on the field or went to the park. Street games, especially skipping and rounders, were a big part of my life and I have never forgotten those times. I loved the rhymes, the friends I skipped with and the body it gave me – I was tall, skinny, fit and healthy. The boys played football, rugby and a little cricket.

As children we had many shared bikes. Mum's red racer was a favourite as was the Triang three-wheeler with a lidded boot which we raced against my brother in his wheelchair. We had scooters, too.

I adore lasagne, mangoes, decaf tea, Veda Bread and Granny's Irish chicken and vegetable broth with freshly made bread. *I am no longer skinny!*

My husband and I, (*I sound like the Queen*) enjoy the odd holiday, mostly cruising to exotic destinations. My favourites include: the UAE, China, Australia, the Caribbean and Japan. Fortunately, we missed the Covid-19 outbreak on the Diamond Princess in Yokohama as it came a few months after our return to the UK. It was very sad watching the ship docked in Japan with so many people infected on board. A very difficult time for passengers, staff and the cruise industry itself. Although I love to travel, I am a home bird at heart. We should have been cruising around the British Isles with the ship docking in Belfast, but the Corona Virus has put paid to that along with Lockdown. Perhaps we might be able to do it in a year's time. However, being safe is crucial and I am staying in!

Hampshire is an amazing place to live and work: I love our village, but I have never forgotten my roots in Belfast and Co. Down, Northern Ireland. I gave birth to my son while living in Coventry.

Millisle, Ballycopeland, Ballywalter and Donaghadee were very important to me as all our school holidays were spent with Granny and Grandad who lived right on the beach in Millisle.

We would fish, swim, even if wet, take boats out, climb the rocks and collect dulse, an edible seaweed, to dry on the shed roof. It cost 3d a bag if bought locally but we enjoyed wading out to the dulse rocks during low tide and having it for free. Sadly a skill or experience none of my children or grandchildren are likely to have.

We made sand houses reinforcing the seats with slates and collected bottles to get the penny deposit back from The First & Last pub. The money was spent on ice cream and Benny's amusements.

Our cousins lived nearby – *'up the road towards Ballycopeland'* and a few miles away in Donaghadee, but we also met people from many destinations in the UK, Europe and America.

Millisle was a sought after holiday resort with families coming for the month of August or a week in a caravan. We'd walk for miles, play ball and board games, cards, skip and read for hours on end. *Reading is something I still do daily.*

Millisle was absolute Heaven for eight weeks every summer. The memories are unforgettable. We loved it!

Elsie O'Neill

AFTERWORD

Many thanks for reading *Beatrice Shilling - A Girl With Grit!*

I first came across Beatrice while teaching and exploring WWII with my Year 3/4s in Hampshire many years ago. They absolutely adored the topic. A wonderful reconstruction was our *'evacuation'* by train to another school in the city, where we carried out wartime activities including writing postcards home, cooking and drama as the 'bombs hit'. Dressed in wartime style outfits and carrying 'gas masks' as well as an authentic packed lunch wrapped in greaseproof paper, we were admired and questioned by many as we walked to the station and back. Beatrice was born a few miles away from where we lived – a real bonus. Sadly she wasn't known to many, if any, locals at all.

I believed it was important to get Beatrice's achievements in the public domain but didn't believe a traditional history book would necessarily appeal to the Tweens and Teens who are our future. Hence linking Jessica's determination, love of bikes, musical theatre and water sports as well as television and internet work to appeal. Much more detail appears in the fuller version of this book: *Beatrice & Jessica – This Girl Can!* This current abridged version mainly deals with Beatrice, because Lockdown has resulted in delays in obtaining permission to use additional TTNY photos.

It was essential to get Beatrice 'out there' now!

Our children must be proud of their accomplishments without being conceited or arrogant. I am certainly very proud of what Jessica has achieved, yet she keeps it quiet.

Bertie has appeared in several adverts, but at five plus does not want to participate anymore. Boys' toys have him hooked along with football at school, but he is still on the agents' books just in case.

STEM (STEaM) exploration and teaching is essential for both boys and girls and we need to encourage it to ensure we develop the right technology and expertise within the UK and across the world. *Female participation is crucial.*

Equal opportunities and gender issues require addressing too. They were problematic one hundred years ago and really should be sorted by 2021.

Nature or nurture is a difficult one. However, families and educators need to guarantee we provide ample STEM type experiences equally to boys and girls. Jessica may enjoy some of her *'girlie'* lifestyle, but also loves being a tom-boy and has explored STEM from an early age. *I am dreading the day she gets a NORTON!*

Some boys may prefer not to dance or act, but follow traditional male roles – no problem there – but they require all round experiences to help them decide. Bertie did dancing for a few years but no longer wishes to do it. He is not so keen on acting or modelling either, but loves big, bad wolf drama activities at home. *Nature or nurture?*

What next?

As previously mentioned, *Traditional Skipping Songs with Jessica and Grandma,* is available on Amazon. *Beatrice & Jessica –*

This Girl Can as well as *Grandma's DNA & Other Stuff*, were put on hold to do the skipping book during the first Lockdown, but should be available in 2021.

Jessica and I are planning a Cook Book, too. She has many recipes and skills for making biscuits, cakes and sweets which sell fast to raise funds for charities and schools. We *must* share them with you! My favourite is her white chocolate covered peppermint and coconut snowballs. *Try out her recipe for the family sponge cake.*

The image shows one plate of several made for a Children in Need fund raising cake stall at school a few years ago. Just a quick snap as we never envisaged writing a cook book at that stage and requiring a good photograph. Once Lockdown is over we can make some more and aim for a better photograph.

Tiny petit fours which are totally irresistible and not a raw egg in sight!
Be aware of those with nut allergies – leave out the coconut!

Grandma says,
"A little bit of what you fancy, now and again,
does you good!"
Not, too often, though.

Oil-based sponge cake – Jessica's recipe

Adapted from Great, Great Grandma's recipe!

Metric/imperial conversions approximate.

Oil based cakes are healthier and lighter than butter based cakes: also easier to make.

Traditionally eggs would be weighed then the same weight in flour, fat and sugar would be used.

Before preparing cakes:

Pre-heat oven to 170°C or gas mark 3

Grease two 20cm baking tins

Ingredients:

225g (8oz) of self-raising flour (sifted)

2 tsps of baking powder

225g (8oz) caster sugar (or grind granulated)

160ml (5.5 fluid oz/9tbsp) of sunflower or rapeseed type cooking oil

3 – 4 large eggs

4 drops of vanilla essence if desired

Buttercream icing or whipped double cream for filling

Chocolate drops or other decorations if desired

Can substitute raspberry or strawberry jam if a Victoria sandwich preferred

Icing sugar or extra caster to dust cake

Buttercream filling/topping

100g (3.50z) unsalted butter

200g (7oz) icing sugar

1 - 2 tbsp fresh milk

Method:

1. Sieve the flour and baking powder into a bowl

2. Add the remainder of cake ingredients – sugar, oil, eggs and essence

3. Mix either by hand, whisk or electric food mixer until smooth and creamy in texture

4. Divide the mixture between the two pre-greased tins

5. Cook for approximately 30 minutes or until golden brown

6. Test by carefully inserting a skewer into the centre of the cake – if it comes out clean it is ready; and/or press finger lightly on top of cake and if no indent it should be cooked.

7. Leave to cool in tin then turn out on wire rack

8. Whip double cream or make buttercream icing to fill as preferred.

Buttercream icing:

1. Beat butter until soft and creamy (works best at room temperature in a warmed bowl)

2. Add 1 tbsp milk, mix slowly

3. Sift and add icing sugar slowly

4. Mix until smooth and creamy, adding more milk if need be

5. Butter one half of cooled cake reserving some for decorating the top as desired

Jessica cut out a circle off the centre of top cake & filled it with buttercream & chocolate drops.

tpsp = teaspoon
tbsp. = tablespoon = 1 ounce

Jessica baking at home during Lockdown in
March 2020

Printed in Great Britain
by Amazon

59040109R00078